Th
Hom
Co

KEEPING KIDS
HEALTHY

THE FAMILY
HOME REMEDIES
COLLECTION

KEEPING KIDS HEALTHY

Cures and remedies for
childhood illnesses and conditions

BY THE EDITORS OF
PREVENTION MAGAZINE HEALTH BOOKS

Rodale Press, Emmaus, Pennsylvania

Prevention is a registered trademark of Rodale Press, Inc.

Printed in the United States of America on recycled ♻ paper

Book Packager: Sandra J. Taylor
Cover and Book Designer: Eugenie Seidenberg Delaney

Library of Congress Cataloging-in-Publication Data

Keeping kids healthy : cures and remedies for childhood illnesses and
    conditions / by the editors of Prevention Magazine Health Books.
        p.   cm. — (The Family home remedies collection)
    Includes index.
    ISBN 0–87596–264–5 paperback
    1. Children—Health and hygiene. 2. Children—Diseases.
3. Pediatrics—Popular works. I. Prevention Magazine Health Books.
II. Series.
RJ61.K26   1995
618.92—dc20   94–24200
                                                       CIP

Distributed in the book trade by St. Martin's Press

2 4 6 8 10 9 7 5 3 1   paperback

OUR MISSION

We publish books that empower people's lives.

RODALE 🏵 BOOKS

NOTICE

This book is intended as a reference volume only, not as a medical guide or manual for self-treatment. If you suspect that you have a medical problem, please seek competent medical care. The information here is designed to help you make informed choices about your health. It is not intended as a substitute for any treatment prescribed by your doctor.

CONTENTS

AGGRESSIVENESS

Many children go through a period—between the ages of two and four—when hitting, kicking and biting are forms of communication, often their only way of saying, "I'm angry" or "I want that." Without the language or social skills to get what they want, they're likely to express their frustration with flying fists or sharp baby teeth.

Although it's a normal developmental stage, aggression can become a way of life. Kids who don't learn to replace their violent eruptions with more civilized behavior, such as sharing, turn-taking and verbal negotiating, often go on to become full-time bullies, says James Bozigar, a licensed social worker and coordinator of community relations for the Family Intervention Center at Children's Hospital of Pittsburgh. Fighting gets them the things they want but makes them feared and unpopular.

If your child is going through this phase, he'll probably get over it before long. But just to nudge his progress a bit, here are a few techniques to help your child curb his aggressive tendencies.

Love that victim. If you witness your preschool child striking another, make your first move toward his victim, advises Robert Mendelson, M.D., clinical professor of pediatrics at Oregon Health Sciences University in Portland. "Pick up the victim. Say, 'Jimmy didn't mean to hurt you.' Give the victim a big hug and kiss, and take him out of the room."

What you are doing is depriving your child of attention, a playmate and you, all at the same time. Suddenly, his fun is gone and he's alone. "It usually doesn't take more than two or three responses like that until the aggressor realizes that being the aggressor isn't in his best interest," says Dr. Mendelson.

Lay down the law. Early on, get your toddler used to the idea of rules. "Just say, 'We don't hit, we don't hurt,'" says Lottie Mendelson, R.N., a pediatric nurse practitioner in Portland, Oregon, and coauthor of *The Complete Book of Parenting*, with her husband Robert. With children aged four and over, the law can be a little more detailed. "You can say, 'In our house, the rule is: If you want a toy, you ask for it, and if the person doesn't give it to you, you wait,'" suggests Bozigar.

Be their guardian angel. Children who strike out physically often cannot control their tempers. For example, when another child has a toy he wants, a hot-tempered child is likely to act impulsively and wrestle it away. He may need to be reminded frequently about the rules you've set.

"Be his adjunct ego or guardian angel," says William Sobesky, Ph.D., assistant clinical professor of psychiatry at the University of Colorado Health Sciences Center and research psychologist at Children's Hospital, both in Denver. "When a child's aggression starts to escalate, point out to him what he is doing and give him alternatives. Say, 'In this situation you may feel like hitting, but that's not okay. You can tell me you're angry. You can tell me you feel like hitting, but it's not okay to do it.'"

Beware the mouth that roars. Don't overlook verbal aggression—it's often the start of something bigger. "A child can have a mouth that 'pushes a button,' causing a playmate to strike back," says Lottie Mendelson. When that happens, be careful not to blame the hitter and allow the instigator to go free. The child who speaks aggressively and starts throwing "verbal punches" should also be reprimanded, she notes.

Call a time-out. A cooling-off period is often the most effective way to change bad behavior. Bozigar says younger children should be placed on a chair away from all distractions for two to three minutes, and older children should be sent to their rooms.

"Just don't do it in a punitive way," he says. "Make it clear you're taking this action because you want things to work out and you want everyone to be happy. Say, 'You can't stop hitting, and I want you to have control of that. So I'm going to help you. I'm going to give you time-out for two or three minutes until you're in control on the inside.'"

Praise good efforts. When children respond in an appropriate way, make sure to reinforce it. "Tell them, 'I like the way you did that,'" says Bozigar. Kids respond better to praise that reflects how their behavior makes their parents feel.

"Saying 'good boy' or 'good girl' is often lost on children," he says. "It's better to say, 'It made me feel so great on the inside when I saw you sharing with your little brother, instead of hitting him. It made me feel I could trust you with him.' That kind of praise is very meaningful to children. It makes them feel that they've had an impact on you."

Create scenarios for success. A child who bullies others learns very quickly that physical aggression has only limited success. It may get him the toy he wants or a turn on the swing, but he's likely to find himself friendless and lonely. He may be very motivated to work on other alternatives.

"You want kids to develop critical thinking skills," says Bozigar. First, talk about what happens when the child uses aggression. "If your child is always beating up other kids at the playground, you can say, 'What happens to you when you do that?' He may say, 'I get into trouble with the playground monitor, the principal calls me into his office and I have detention.' Then you can say, 'That's not a success for you. What can we do to give you a success?' Kids really respond to that."

Once the child realizes he's getting in trouble, you can start him thinking about possible solutions, Bozigar points out. For example, if he's being aggressive on the playground, you might want to practice different ways of getting involved in activities. Urge him to ask nicely whether he can join in—or to toss a ball back from out-of-bounds until the other kids ask him to play.

Use a scrapbook to scrap bad behavior. With a younger child who's beginning to show signs of aggressiveness, Bozigar recommends that you make up a little storybook with the child as the hero. Using pictures cut from magazines or photographs of the child himself, show situations where the child uses verbal or other problem-solving skills to deal with his frustration.

Talk with him about these options. "Do it at a time when the child is not in the midst of emotional turmoil," he says. "When those emotions are up, it's hard to bring them down."

Share the fantasy. One technique that is often effective in helping children gain a new perspective on their behavior is to grant in fantasy what you can't in real life, says Bozigar. "A child who thinks he should have the playground all to himself can have it—in fantasy. Say, 'Okay, for the rest of the week, Tommy is the only one who is allowed on the playground. No one is allowed on the swings but Tommy, and everyone is going to have to stand around and applaud.'"

Once Tommy sees that his wildest dreams are just that—and funny, to boot—bring him back to earth. "Say, 'Yeah, that sounds cool, but in real life you have to *share* the playground. So let's talk about another way we can make this a success for you,'" says Bozigar.

Use force as the last resort. Forceful restraint should be used only when a child is putting himself or someone else in danger, says Dr. Sobesky. "If you must use physical restraint, approach the child from behind, pulling his arms down. Wrap your legs around his legs and keep your chin away from his head."

Be aware that restraint may increase rage in some children. "But others may find it reassuring that you can control them," says Dr. Sobesky. "Just make sure you hold your child in a comforting, nonaggressive way so he doesn't feel he's being attacked."

ATTENTION PROBLEMS

Your son sits down to start his homework, but his attention is distracted by the rustling of a tree outside his window. So he stares out the window a while. Then he jumps up to play with a toy truck. On the way back to his desk, he stops to tickle his little brother.

So why can't he sit still long enough to finish a task? His short attention span may seem like an unconquerable problem. But experts say there are things you can do to help your child focus better.

Confer with the teacher. "If your child's attention problems occur only at school, there may be a teacher problem," says Cynthia Whitham, a licensed clinical social worker and staff therapist at the Parent Training Clinic at the University of California, Los Angeles, and author of *Win the Whining War and Other Skirmishes.* If this is the case, arrange a conference with the teacher to discuss the problem and possible solutions.

Check out home stressors. If the problems occur only at home, they could be a reaction to home stressors. "If you see distractibility, overactivity and impulsiveness in your child, and you're going through separation, divorce or other troublesome times, the behavior might be temporary," says Whitham. She suggests increasing time with your child to give her opportunities to express her feelings to you.

Arrange a hearing check. If your child is inattentive and easily distracted, but not overactive or impulsive, consider having him screened for hearing problems or auditory processing problems, suggests Sam Goldstein, Ph.D., a child psychologist who is a clinical instructor at the University of Utah School of Medicine and codirector of the Neurology, Learning and Behavior Center in Salt Lake City. "Though he may hear you, it's possible that all the information he's hearing isn't reaching his brain effectively," he says.

CUT DOWN ON ADDITIVES

A number of studies indicate that there is a connection between childhood attention problems and the chemical additives in processed food. According to one study, the behavior of more than half of a group of hyperactive children deteriorated markedly when they were exposed to artificial flavorings, colors and preservatives. Their behavior improved when the additives were removed.

While some authorities disagree about the exact role of additives with respect to attentional difficulties and hyperactivity, "it certainly can't hurt and very possibly may help to eliminate chemical additives as much as possible from your child's diet," says John F. Taylor, Ph.D., a family psychologist in Salem, Oregon, and author of *Helping Your Hyperactive Child.*

For information on common additives and how to avoid them, contact the Feingold Association, P.O. Box 6550, Alexandria, VA 22306.

Heighten the fun level. Build the following elements into as many of your child's activities as possible: movement, novelty, variety, color, skin contact and excitement. When helping with spelling, for example, have your child print the words with crayons onto three-by-five-inch cards rather than merely spelling them out loud. The cards can be used for drill and review. To sustain attention during chores, play lively music and join the child in dancelike movements. "If the activity has an intrinsic appeal to a distractible child, his attention span will be longer," says John F. Taylor, Ph.D., a family psychologist in Salem, Oregon, and author of *Helping Your Hyperactive Child.*

Turn the desk. A child who's easily distracted will be able to focus on homework and other tasks more easily and for longer periods if his desk chair faces a wall rather than an open room or a window, says Dr. Taylor.

Frame and focus. Cut a large piece of cardboard into a shape like a picture frame and place it around the "attention area" on your child's desk, suggests Dr. Taylor. Tell her to look inside the picture frame to do her work. This will help her concentrate, according to Dr. Taylor.

Make eye contact. To improve communication with your inattentive child, always make eye contact with her before you speak, suggests Whitham.

Tell, don't ask. Get in the habit of using statements, not questions. "A short series of commands is much easier to follow," says Whitham. For example, don't say, "Can't you find your jacket, honey?" Instead, say, "Go find your jacket now, and come back and show me."

Be specific. "Provide positive directions," says Dr. Goldstein. Instead of telling your child what *not* to do, tell him what *to* do. Don't say, "Take your feet off that chair." Instead, say, "Put your feet on the floor." Otherwise, your child may remove his feet from the chair but do something equally distracting, such as putting his feet on the bookcase.

Make a list. Make and post a list or chart of tasks your child can check off or cross out when completed, says Whitham. "That way, you won't have to repeat yourself because the chart gives the reminder," she explains. If the tasks aren't getting done, calmly tell your child to go check his list.

Give credit for trying. Have patience with your inattentive child: She may be doing her best. "Many children have trouble starting a task and sticking to it," says Dr. Goldstein. "This is not behavior which they can easily control or stop, just because you repeatedly tell them to."

Choose your battles. Child development experts often recommend ignoring your child when his behavior is something you don't like but can tolerate. Eventually your child will stop the troublesome behavior because he's not getting any attention for it. "The trick is to *always* pay attention to your child when he stops the behavior you don't like and starts the behavior you *do* like," says Dr. Goldstein.

Be consistent. "Set up and stick to schedules and routines," suggests Dr. Goldstein. "Children with attention problems often benefit from consistent routines, including specific time periods for watching television, doing homework, playing, performing chores and eating dinner." Minimize disruptions. When interruptions are unavoidable, however, try to warn your child ahead of time that there's going to be a change of schedule.

Supply a release. To keep your child on a task longer, Dr. Taylor suggests you allow ways she can incorporate some movement into her work. For instance, give her a sponge rubber ball, a ball of colorful yarn or a colorful shoelace to squeeze or fiddle with while working.

Consider the sugar connection. While research findings don't thoroughly condemn sugar, according to Dr. Taylor, he believes parents should consider cutting down on their child's intake. "After diagnosing and treating about 1,400 children, I've found that somewhere around a third of the parents have told me that food with high sugar content causes their child's behavior to deteriorate significantly," says Dr. Taylor.

He adds that some research has shown that giving a high-protein food can block the effect of sugar in children sensitive to it. So if your child eats a sugary meal such as pancakes and syrup, supply a protein source such as yogurt, peanut butter, eggs or cheese.

BED-WETTING

Sally, age four, routinely wakes up in the mornings with a wet bed. Joe is five years older. But even at age nine, he tries to stay awake all night whenever he sleeps over at a friend's house. He's still terrified he will wet the bed in his sleep.

Sally and Joe share a common childhood problem: bed-wetting. About one in five 4- and 5-year-olds wets the bed, and as many as one in ten boys still has a problem by age 12. (For some reason, it's more common in boys than girls.)

"It's not unusual for children not to be dry at night at age four and five, and some of us really don't consider it something that should be treated until a child is at least six," says George Sterne, M.D., clinical professor of pediatrics at Tulane University Medical School and a pediatrician in private practice in New Orleans.

There may be some kind of physical problem or health condition that's causing your child to wet the bed. If you're concerned about that, you should definitely discuss your child's bed-wetting with a doctor. But usually bed-wetting can be cured without medical intervention, given enough time along with a healthy dose of patience. Here are the techniques the experts recommend.

Rid yourself—and Junior—of guilt. Realize that you're not a bad parent because your child wets the bed, and make it clear to your child that he isn't a bad child because he wets. "Bed-wetting is a biological problem. It occurs in a child who, during sleep, has not learned bladder control skills," says Barton D. Schmitt, M.D., director of consultative services at the Ambulatory Care Center at Children's Hospital of Denver and author of *Your Child's Health.*

"I think it's so important to tell parents of bed wetters that this is *rarely* a psychological problem," says Dr. Schmitt. "There's a lot of unnecessary guilt imposed on some very good parents because they see themselves as being somehow to blame."

Ban punishments. One study found that nearly three-fourths of parents punished their children for bed-wetting. Never punish or scold your child for a wet bed, says Thomas Bartholomew, M.D., a pediatric urologist and assistant professor of surgery and urology at the University of Texas Health Science Center at San Antonio. "Parents should understand that this is not going to help their child," says Dr. Bartholomew. "I've never met a child who *wants* to wet the bed."

Protect with plastic. A zip-up plastic mattress cover should be standard equipment on any bed wetter's bed. It protects the mattress, of course. But also it means there's less of a "crisis" when the child wets the bed, Dr. Schmitt points out. Both parents and kids will stay calmer if they know there's not much clean-up to worry about.

Encourage clean-up duties. You should, however, matter-of-factly tell the child he is expected to clean up the wet bed or at least help. "Even at age four and five a child can take the sheets off the bed and put them in the laundry room," says Lottie Mendelson, R.N., a pediatric nurse practitioner in Portland, Oregon, and coauthor of *The Complete Book of Parenting*. "It should not be punitive, just an acknowledgment that this is the child's responsibility. It also helps you. That way, you don't feel the child is doing this *to* you."

Check out your child's motivation. Before taking active steps to cure bed-wetting, make sure your child *wants* to stop, says Jeffrey Fogel, M.D., a pediatrician in private practice in Fort Washington, Pennsylvania, and staff physician at Chestnut Hill Hospital in Philadelphia. "When a parent asks me how to cure bed-wetting I ask, 'Does your child want to be dry?' If they say 'no,' I say, 'You can try all you want, but you probably won't be successful.'" If a child wants to stop, she'll not only cooperate, but her conscious mind will also work on her subconscious to help her awaken at night, explains Dr. Fogel.

Recognize the signs. A child often becomes motivated to stop wetting when it begins to interfere with his social options, says Dr. Bartholomew. When the child starts to refuse invitations to spend the night away from home, or doesn't go to camp because of bed-wetting fears, you can point out the benefits of being able to do these things. Then suggest some ways your child can help himself get through the night with a dry bed.

Pick a good time. Before starting, choose a relatively peaceful period—not, for example, just before an exciting holiday or vacation, advises Cathleen Piazza, Ph.D., assistant professor of psychiatry at Johns Hopkins University School of Medicine and chief psychologist of the neurobehavioral unit at Kennedy Krieger Institute in Baltimore. "You should pick a time when you're not having multiple stressors at work and in the household," she says.

Keep bedtimes calm. Lots of rough-housing or even an exciting television program close to bedtime can increase the risk of bed-wetting, says Patrick Holden, M.D., associate professor of psychiatry at the University of Texas Health Science Center at San Antonio. "When kids are excited they tend to produce more urine," he explains. Instead of letting your child watch television before bedtime, give him a book to read, have a quiet conversation or read a story to him.

Put the child in charge. You want your child to understand from the outset that staying dry at night is his responsibility. That means *don't* waken your child at night to take him to the bathroom.

"Waking the child doesn't teach him anything about bladder control, and it's probably counterproductive," says Dr. Schmitt. "If the child goes to bed thinking his parent is going to wake him up at night, that's teaching the child that the parent is going to take care of his bladder and that he doesn't have to worry about it. Your child has to go to bed just a little bit worried to stay dry."

Reward dry nights. Consistently reward or congratulate your child when she has made it through the night with a dry bed. "You'll get a lot further if you give positive psychological support such as hugs and warm congratulations," says Dr. Bartholomew. Some kids might like happy faces drawn on a calendar or special stickers, says Dr. Piazza. Whatever reinforcement you use, do it first thing in the morning.

Make getting up easy. Some kids are reluctant to leave their beds, and others have been ordered by parents never to get up after they've been tucked in, says Dr. Schmitt. "So you need to give your kids permission to get up to go to the bathroom. They need a flashlight or a night-light, and they need to be asked if they want a potty chair next to their bed. Some kids who don't want to go to the bathroom are perfectly willing to use the potty chair and go back to sleep."

Give your child an alarm clock. If the child has a regular pattern of wetting the bed at the same time every night, furnish an alarm clock and explain how it works, says Barbara Howard, M.D., assistant clinical professor of pediatrics at Duke University Medical Center in Durham, North Carolina. "The child can set the alarm clock to wake him up 20 minutes to half an hour before he usually wets the bed so he can get up and go to the bathroom," she explains.

Avoid caffeine. Caffeine is a diuretic, a substance that encourages urination, explains Dr. Howard. It's in many sodas and in chocolate as well as in coffee and tea. Avoiding these foods and drinks may help your child avoid wetting, she says.

Encourage bladder-control practice. Explain to your child that she can help "train" her bladder by practicing during the day. Have your child drink a lot, and then wait as long as she can to go to the bathroom. "Have her try to wait a little bit longer each time," says Dr. Piazza. "You want to train a child to associate the feeling of having a full bladder with having to go to the bathroom."

Stream-interruption exercises can also help, says Dr. Schmitt. Have the child begin to urinate and then stop briefly before starting up again. She should try to do this several times each time she urinates. "Those exercises build up the bladder sphincter," says Dr. Schmitt.

Buy a bed alarm. Most experts agree that moisture-activated bed alarms are the most effective treatment for bed-wetting. Alarms are battery-operated, cost around $40 and are available from several companies without a prescription. Ask your pediatrician to recommend a brand or type. Use the alarm until your child is dry every night for one month. In most alarms, wetting triggers a loud sound that awakens the child. A silent, vibrating alarm is also available for children who don't respond to sound.

Dr. Schmitt recommends portable, transistorized alarms that are worn on the body rather than the bell and pad devices. And he says parents shouldn't insist on using the alarm if the child is opposed to it.

BRONCHITIS

Just when your child is getting over a cold or the flu, his temperature starts to climb and he begins to have coughing fits and spit up mucus. When you take him to the doctor, you're likely to hear one of those "-itis" words, which means something is inflamed.

In this case, the -itis is bronchitis, and it means inflammation of the bronchial tubes, the two large tubes that branch off the windpipe. Bronchitis can be caused by wayward bacteria from the throat or by the same virus that caused the initial cold or flu. As the lining of those tubes swells, mucus builds up. The heavy coughing is a sign that your child is trying to clear that mucus from his bronchial passages.

If the bronchitis is caused by bacteria, your doctor may pre-scribe an antibiotic. If it's a viral infection, an antibiotic won't help, but there's a lot you can do to make your child more comfortable and maybe even get over it faster. Here are some home-remedy tac-tics that doctors recommend for both bacterial and viral bronchitis.

Give extra fluids. Water is best, but any liquid will do, says F. T. Fitzpatrick, M.D., a pediatrician in private practice in Doylestown, Pennsylvania. The fluids help thin the mucus, making it easier to cough up, and can also soothe a throat that's tickly from coughing. An eight-year-old child should drink at least four eight-ounce glasses of liquid a day.

Moisturize the bedroom. Humidity may help soothe the irritated bronchial membranes, says J. Owen Hendley, M.D., pro-fessor of pediatrics and head of pediatric infectious diseases at the University of Virginia School of Medicine in Charlottesville. Close the door to your child's bedroom, turn on the vaporizer about a half hour before he goes to sleep and leave it on all night, he says. "That way you can get the humidity up to as much as 70 percent."

Encourage productive coughing. Since the mucus in the bronchial tubes is causing your child to cough, encourage her to clear her lungs, says Dr. Hendley. If a small child is having trouble coughing up the mucus, pat her gently on the back. Keep tissues available so that your child can use them if needed.

Use a prop. Use an extra pillow at night to help prop up your child while he sleeps, suggests Mary Meland, M.D., a pediatrician with HealthPartners in Bloomington, Minnesota. Propping up his head helps him breathe more easily.

Soothe with chicken soup. Mom's chicken soup is more than comforting to an ill child; it really does help clear congestion. "Some scientific evidence has shown that chicken soup helps clear secretions better than other liquids," says Dr. Meland.

Nix the smoking. Don't allow anyone to smoke in your house, says Dr. Fitzpatrick. If you smoke, go outside to do it. The smoke irritates the bronchial tubes and can make the infection worse.

Try an expectorant. Over-the-counter expectorants that contain guaifenesin such as Robitussin, Triaminic Expectorant and many others *may* help loosen the mucus so that coughing can work to clear the bronchial passages, says Dr. Hendley. There's no hard scientific proof that they work, he says, but there's no harm in trying one. Read the label carefully and give a dose suitable for your child's age.

Consider a cough suppressant at night. If your child is coughing so much she can't get any rest, it's okay to use a cough suppressant at night, says William Howatt, M.D., professor of pediatrics in the Department of Pediatrics and Communicable Diseases at the University of Michigan Medical Center in Ann Arbor. Robitussin Pediatric Cough Suppressant may help—and other over-the-counter suppressants for children are available at drugstores. Try to avoid giving the suppressants during the day if your child has productive coughing. That coughing is *needed* to help clear the bronchial tubes.

CHICKEN POX

At first your child just doesn't feel well. "Sorta tired" is all he can tell you. When you put him to bed, you notice one little bump on his tummy—maybe a bug bite, you think.

In the morning, that little bump has been joined by a flock of others, and some of them show tiny clear water blisters.

Say hello to the chicken pox.

It's a fairly harmless malady that can strike adults as well as babies and children. For a week or more, the discomfort is almost continual. First there may be mild fever, then blisters, itching and finally scabbing. In very rare cases, chicken pox can lead to more serious ailments.

For parents, this uncomfortable malady offers just one consolation: After your child has had it, chicken pox is gone for good. (Unless, that is, you have another susceptible child in the house who hasn't been through it before.)

Here's how the experts suggest you keep your child with chicken pox as comfortable as possible.

Supply pain relief. If the fever or itching is making your child unbearably uncomfortable, you can give her acetaminophen, says William Howatt, M.D., professor of pediatrics in the Department of Pediatrics and Communicable Diseases at the University of Michigan Medical Center in Ann Arbor. Check the package directions for the correct dosage for your child's age and weight. If your child is under age two, consult a physician. If the fever isn't making your child uncomfortable, however, don't try to lower it: "It's actually one of the body's disease-fighting mechanisms," explains Dr. Howatt.

Dress your child lightly. "The cooler you can keep your child's skin in the first 48 to 72 hours, the less rash he'll have," says F. T. Fitzpatrick, M.D., a pediatrician in private practice in Doylestown, Pennsylvania. Avoid bundling your child up, and dress him lightly in cotton clothing or pajamas.

Cotton is the best choice because it's the least irritating to the skin, says Dr. Fitzpatrick.

Supply cooling relief. Another way to help lower your child's temperature is to bathe her skin with a cool cloth or put her in a cool bath, says J. Owen Hendley, M.D., professor of pediatrics at the University of Virginia School of Medicine at Charlottesville. Be sure the water isn't so cold your child shivers, however.

Try an itch-relieving bath. A bath in colloidal oat-meal—oatmeal that's been ground to a fine powder—can help soothe the itch, says Kenneth R. Keefner, Ph.D., a pharmacist and associate professor of pharmacy in the School of Pharmacy and Allied Health Professions at Creighton University in Omaha. You can find this product at most pharmacies under the brand name Aveeno, and directions for use are on the box. But take special care that your child doesn't try to stand in the bath, because this product can make the bathtub quite slippery, says Dr. Keefner.

Or soothe with soda. Baking soda is a perfectly good substitute for colloidal oatmeal, according to Dr. Keefner. Stir about half a cup of baking soda into a shallow bath or a full cup in a deep bath. Use a washcloth to spread the bath water over all affected areas of skin.

Cool the itchy spots. If your child has one or two spots that are particularly itchy, wring out a washcloth in cool water, lay it on the area for five minutes and repeat as needed. "Coolness on the site of the itch can counteract the itching," says Dr. Hendley. If the cloth is rough on one side, however, put the smooth side next to the skin to avoid irritation, he suggests.

Keep your child fresh and clean. Children with chicken pox should get a daily shower and shampoo to keep the sores clean and help prevent infection, says Dr. Fitzpatrick. Also, while it may be tempting to let your groggy child fall asleep in the same pajamas she's worn all day, she should have a clean pair for the night, he

THE ASPIRIN DANGER

Don't give children aspirin to treat the pain and fever that accompany chicken pox, because aspirin has been associated with Reye's syndrome, a life-threatening neurological disorder. While its cause is unknown, Reye's syndrome is associated with the use of aspirin by children who have viral infections, most often chicken pox or influenza.

Better: Use Tylenol or another acetaminophen preparation for fever, says Edgar O. Ledbetter, M.D., former chairman of the Department of Pediatrics at Texas Tech University in Lubbock.

says. (If your child is still in diapers, they should be changed frequently.) Not only is the clean clothing comforting, but the change can reduce the risk of the sores getting infected.

Try to control the scratching. If your child is old enough to understand, explain that he should try not to scratch because scratching can cause infection or scarring. But chances are your child can't *completely* ignore the raging itch all the time, so supply a cool, wet washcloth he can scratch gently with, suggests Dr. Hendley. "This will help keep him from ripping his skin open," he says.

Clip nails short. Trim your child's fingernails as soon as chicken pox strikes—and keep them trimmed short, says Dr. Fitzpatrick. Even after the worst is over, he recommends trimming the nails twice a week for several weeks afterward. Scratching with sharp nails can lead to a bacterial infection in the sores, and that can lead to permanent scarring.

Treat with an antibiotic. If a few of the pox show signs of infection such as redness around the pox or the presence of pus in an open pox, apply an over-the-counter antibiotic ointment such as Neosporin or Polysporin, says Dr. Keefner. "But if more than a few of the sores are infected, contact your pediatrician," he cautions.

Control the itch with an antihistamine. "An oral over-the-counter antihistamine, like Benadryl Elixir, may help control the itching," says Dr. Hendley. "But even if it doesn't, at least it will make your child sleepy so he can get some of the rest he needs." Be sure to read package directions to make certain the product is recommended for your child's age. For the correct dosage, follow package directions or consult your physician. Some doctors don't advise Benadryl cream or spray because it could cause a reaction.

Or try calamine lotion with phenol. This type of calamine lotion works as a topical anesthetic and can help with the itching, says Edward DeSimone, Ph.D., a pharmacist and associate professor of pharmacy administrative and social sciences in the School of Pharmacy and Allied Health Professions at Omaha's Creighton University. Just dab it on particularly itchy pox. Because this product can be absorbed through the skin, you want to apply it just to the pox—not smear it all over, says Dr. DeSimone. "Also, make sure that you don't exceed package directions, which specify that this lotion should not be used more than three or four times a day."

COLIC

Your baby cries to communicate—to say that he is hungry, wet, cold, lonely, sick or bored. And if he's like most babies, he will also have fussy spells when he cries a lot for no apparent reason.

If your baby has repeated episodes of crying that last for several hours at a time, but sure to consult your pediatrician. He may tell you that your baby has colic.

A colicky baby may cry in a rhythmic pattern that often reaches a screaming level. He may clench his hands, flex his elbows and draw his legs tight against his abdomen. His face may look worried or tense, his belly seems tight and he has lots of gas. Sometimes he has a forceful expulsion of gas or a bowel movement right before or right after the bout of colic.

As many as one in five babies develops colic, yet it remains something of a medical mystery. Colic has been blamed on many things, including a hypersensitive nervous system, an immature gastrointestinal tract, food allergy and improper feeding technique. Although there is no consensus about the cause and treatment of this ailment, one thing is certain: Colic typically strikes otherwise healthy babies at the age of 2 to 3 weeks and is usually over by the time the baby is 12 to 16 weeks old. And awful as it is to live through, it will not harm your baby in the long run, either physically or psychologically.

There is no surefire cure for colic except time, patience and perseverance, but some parents have found temporary relief by using the following methods.

Take a systematic approach. What helps one colicky baby will do nothing for another, so you'll have to experiment to see what works with your child, says Russell S. Asnes, M.D., clinical professor of pediatrics at the College of Physicians and Surgeons at Columbia University in New York City and a pediatrician in Tenafly, New Jersey. "Take a systematic approach to determine the cause of your baby's cries," urges Dr. Asnes. "Check if he is hungry, wet, cold, wants some extra sucking on a pacifier or wants to be held. If he is warm and dry and has been fed recently, he may want company, so talk to him and rock him. If he is bored, take him out for a walk or a car ride."

No matter which approach you try, change tactics if the crying continues for more than five minutes, says Dr. Asnes. Eventually you should hit on something that will work for your baby.

Take a cue from your baby. If you find that the more you try to comfort your inconsolable child, the more he cries, your baby's colic may be triggered by an overloaded nervous system, notes Peter A. Gorski, M.D., division head of behavioral and developmental pediatrics and assistant professor of pediatrics and psychiatry at Northwestern University Medical School in Chicago.

"If your baby has already had as much stimulation as he can handle, even calming techniques such as rocking, singing and talking softly are too much to take in and only serve to intensify your baby's irritability," says Dr. Gorski. Crying is one way for a baby to "shut out the world," observes Dr. Gorski. So when your usual methods of calming your infant aren't working, let him cry for 10 to 15 minutes and see whether he'll calm down by himself before you try anything else. "Hold the baby passively in your arms, or swaddle him and lay him down to rest," he says. "You may even find that avoiding direct eye contact helps him calm down sooner. After the crying spell, your baby should look wide awake and be ready to interact, or be resting calmly. If not, consult your pediatrician." There may be a hernia or some other physical problem that's causing the prolonged irritability.

Try a regular feeding schedule. "Studies show that excessively sensitive babies are often small for their age. Their length is normal but they are thin. These babies, who indicate sensory overload by having colicky episodes, often do better with an organized pattern of caretaking," says Barry M. Lester, Ph.D., professor of psychiatry and human behavior and professor of pediatrics at Brown University School of Medicine in Providence, Rhode Island. "For some reason, organizing these babies' environment helps them organize their responses. Structure really helps," says Dr. Lester.

Don't count on new formula. Many parents try switching to a soy formula in the hope that this will ease their baby's distress, but Dr. Gorski notes that it is very rare for colicky babies to be intolerant to milk. "A formula change usually gives that classic placebo effect. It may seem to work for a few days, but then it makes no difference," he says.

Check your feeding system. "Make sure that when you nurse or bottlefeed your baby, he is held in an upright rather than a horizontal position, and burp him well," says Dr. Asnes. "This helps prevent him from swallowing too much air, a source of discomfort. Also, if you use a bottle, check the size of the nipple hole. If it is too small, your child may be hungry—and frustrated that he can't get at the formula."

Try motion and music. Some colicky babies get temporary relief if they are swaddled and held next to your chest or carried in a front pack. Others may calm to the sound of music or the vacuum cleaner. "There are many ways to hold and soothe a baby, but there is no universal soothing method. Some techniques that work well for your baby will do nothing for another child," says Dr. Asnes.

COUGHING AT NIGHT

O n Monday your son's sleep was disturbed by a dry, hacking cough. Since then, the cough has been keeping him and everybody else up. Now it's Friday night, and even the dog is howling.

Of course, you are doing your best to ease those nasty night-time symptoms. You've rubbed some strong-smelling ointment on his chest, dosed him with a multi-symptom cough and cold medicine, and turned up the heat in his room. Now you're wondering if you should ask the doctor for some antibiotics. Unfortunately, according to the experts, none of those measures actually helps to stop the coughing.

"The most common reason for a child's night-time coughing is a viral infection," says Blake E. Noyes, M.D., assistant professor of pediatrics in the Division of Pulmonology at Children's Hospital of Pittsburgh. "And that's the kind of illness that can't be treated with antibiotics."

Because coughing is an important mechanism for keeping the lungs clear, you don't want to stop it completely. "If your child has a viral illness, his natural defense mechanisms are temporarily impaired. The cough helps keep the lungs clear of bacteria and other irritants," says Dr. Noyes. "If you suppress the coughing completely, you are wiping away an important defense against a more serious bacterial infection such as pneumonia."

Although in many cases it's best to leave a night-time cough alone, doctors say there are steps you can take, when necessary, to make your child more comfortable.

Offer lots to drink. The traditional recommendation, "Drink plenty of liquids," is still good advice when your child has a cough. "Fluids such as juice, water or clear broth are some of the best expectorants around," says Robert C. Beckerman, M.D., a professor of pediatrics and physiology and section chief of pediatric pulmonology at Tulane University School of Medicine in New Orleans. Fluids can loosen up a dry, hard cough and help expel phlegm. And unlike cold medications, there are no side effects.

"A hot drink, in particular, can be a soothing comfort when your child has a cough," says Dr. Noyes. But any type of drink will do. "When kids get stuffed up, they tend to breathe through the mouth, which dries out the throat and leads to a cough. Just keeping the mouth and throat moist may reduce the coughing," he says.

Turn down the thermostat. If your child's cough strikes during the winter months when the house is heated, you should turn the thermostat down at night, not up. "Hot, dry air will irritate a cough. But if you set the thermostat lower, the cooler air will preserve some humidity," says Naomi Grobstein, M.D., a family physician in private practice in Montclair, New Jersey.

Don't rush to vaporize. Although it seems sensible to add some humidity with a vaporizer, that's not always a good idea. "Vaporizers are hard to keep clean," notes Dr. Beckerman, "and they tend to be a breeding ground for mold and bacteria." If your child is allergic to mold, or is an asthmatic, a vaporizer could make the cough even worse, he says.

Skip the chest rub. "Petroleum products which create a warm feeling on the chest do nothing to ease a cough," says Dr. Beckerman. And if the child inhales or swallows a chest-rub product, it could possibly lead to a form of pneumonia.

Try an antihistamine. If you know that your child's cough is caused by an allergy, an antihistamine at bedtime may help him get some sleep. "Allergic coughs may be helped by over-the-counter drugs such as Benadryl Elixir," says Dr. Beckerman. Be sure to read package directions to make certain the product is recommended for your child's age. For the correct dosage, follow package directions or consult your physician.

Choose the right cough medicine. "If your child has been up for a few nights with a bad cough, you can try a cough medicine containing dextromethorphan and guaifenesin, such as

WHEN COUGHING WON'T QUIT

I t's important that your child be checked by a doctor to determine the cause of any severe or persistent cough, says Blake E. Noyes, M.D., assistant professor of pediatrics in the Division of Pulmonology at Children's Hospital of Pittsburgh. "Nighttime coughing may be due to a virus, a bacterial infection, asthma, something your child swallowed that is partially blocking the airway, irritating fumes or, in some cases, a more serious disease such as cystic fibrosis," he says.

You should consult a physician, advises Dr. Noyes, if your child:

• Coughs continually throughout the night.
• Coughs up phlegm.
• Has a fever.
• Has difficulty breathing.
• Has a cough that has lasted more than ten days.

Robitussin-DM or Vicks Pediatric Formula 44e," says Dr. Grobstein. "Basically, any products with these two ingredients will do," she adds. This type of over-the-counter preparation will loosen up the mucus a bit and provide very mild cough relief. "Dextromethorphan is not 100 percent effective," she says, "but that's actually good because you shouldn't try to suppress a cough entirely."

Caution: Don't give potent cough medication to a child who is under one year of age, says Dr. Beckerman. "The cough reflex is controlled in the brain stem, and if you give a very young child something to suppress it, you might also suppress breathing."

CRADLE CAP

That yellow, dry crust marring the perfect beauty of your infant's scalp may look unsightly. But cradle cap, a common skin inflammation that's most noticeable in infants (though children of all ages are susceptible), is usually not dangerous.

Surprisingly, a mild case of cradle cap isn't even irritating to your baby. But it is worth treating if it starts to spread or grow thicker. So if you see that telltale "cap" appearing like crust on the scalp, here are some easy ways to cope.

Leave it alone. If the cradle cap is mild and confined to the scalp, it can be safely left alone, says Karen Wiss, M.D., assistant professor of medicine and pediatrics and director of pediatric dermatology at the University of Massachusetts Medical Center in Worcester. "Cradle cap may look irritating, but for the most part, it is not bothersome to the baby," she says.

Slack off from shampooing. "Wash your baby's hair no more than every other day, using a gentle baby shampoo. Overwashing has a drying effect and can aggravate cradle cap," says Luisa Castiglia, M.D., a pediatrician in private practice in Mineola, New York.

Use a toothbrush. If you do want to do something about cradle cap, scalp brushing may help. "At the first sign of cradle cap, parents should use a drop of baby oil or cooking oil to loosen up the flakes on the baby's scalp and then lightly brush the scalp with a soft toothbrush. This loosens a lot of scale, which can then be removed by shampooing your baby's hair with regular baby shampoo," says Fran E. Adler, M.D., a pediatrician in private practice in Upper Montclair, New Jersey. This treatment is not a quick fix, but if you persist, you may see gradual improvement.

Switch shampoos. If the scale becomes very thick, it can be annoying to your infant and may even become infected, notes

Dr. Wiss. She suggests shampooing the baby's hair twice a week with an over-the-counter dandruff shampoo such as Sebulex. "Use a small amount of shampoo, and avoid getting it into the baby's eyes. It won't harm the eyes, but it will sting," says Dr. Wiss.

Dr. Adler adds that you'll get the most out of the dandruff shampoo treatment by keeping the lather on for five minutes before rinsing.

Try a special liquid. For very thick cradle cap, Dr. Wiss recommends loosening the scale by using Baker's P & S Liquid, a mild, mineral-oil-based solution available at drugstores. "Apply the P & S Liquid at night, comb through the scale with a fine-toothed comb and wash it out in the morning," she says.

"The baby's fontanelle [the soft spot on the skull] is a delicate area, but it won't be damaged by gentle combing and brushing," adds Dr. Castiglia.

Watch out for creeping. If cradle cap starts creeping down behind your baby's ears and onto the neck, it definitely needs treatment, notes Dr. Adler. If your doctor okays it, treat the affected areas with 0.5 percent or 1 percent hydrocortisone cream, which is available over-the-counter. If you apply the cream three times a day, it should clear up that crust immediately, she says. Be sure to consult your pediatrician, however, because this is strong medication, according to Dr. Adler.

CRANKINESS

When kids turn cranky, a lot of parents take it personally. "He's just doing it to get his way" is one interpretation of Johnny's pouts and whines. Some kids are *temperamentally* cranky, suggests William Sobesky, Ph.D., assistant clinical professor of psychiatry at the University of Colorado Health Sciences Center and research psychologist at Children's Hospital, both in Denver. "You don't need to think of it as intentional or take it personally. It's just the way the child is wired."

But other kids do use crankiness as a form of manipulation. They quickly learn that "Mommy hates it when I whine and cry at the mall, so she buys me a chocolate chip cookie." Here are a few tips to head off crankiness *before* it becomes a habit.

If there's a problem, take care of it. Perhaps the most common cause of crankiness is a physical need. "The child is tired or hungry or bored," says Dr. Sobesky. "Give her time for a nap or, if you're out, put her on your shoulder. Get her something to eat or distract her."

Don't respond to whining. "If your child uses whining to get your attention, say very simply, 'I don't understand you when you're whining,'" suggests Robert Mendelson, M.D., a pediatrician and clinical professor of pediatrics at Oregon Health Sciences University in Portland. "Tell the child, 'When you're ready, come and tell me what's bothering you and then we'll talk about it.' As soon as the whining stops, say, 'I'm glad you're feeling better.'"

Pay attention to the good stuff. Kids who are using crankiness to get attention should get attention for other, more pleasant things they do. "The child who is picked up every time she smiles, coos and gurgles learns that when she wants attention all she has to do is smile, coo and gurgle," says Dr. Mendelson. "Don't reward negative behavior by giving her attention *only* when she's cranky. If you do, you'll just see more of that behavior."

Raise a do-it-yourselfer. Kids use crankiness and whining as a way of saying *"Do this for me!"*

"They whine because they can't tie shoes, their blocks fall down, they don't want to go to bed or they don't want to eat. Whining is a flag that is signaling, 'Please teach me some skills,'" says Edward Christophersen, Ph.D., clinical psychologist at Children's Mercy Hospital and professor of pediatrics at the University of Missouri–Kansas City School of Medicine.

Rather than leaping to their aid at the first whine, give them some time to figure out what to do on their own, suggests Dr. Christophersen. If they need some instruction, make your explanations brief and simple—and make it clear you're confident they can do the task themselves. "The more you help," warns Dr. Christophersen, "the more dependent children become."

Explain the facts of life. With older children, explain that their crankiness is working against them, suggests Lottie Mendelson, R.N., a pediatric nurse practitioner in Portland, Oregon, and coauthor of *The Complete Book of Parenting*, with her husband, Robert. If you tell the child how annoying it is when she's constantly cranky, she'll be able to understand how crankiness affects other people.

CROUP

Your child has had the sniffles for a few days when suddenly he wakes up in the middle of the night with a strange cough that sounds like a seal barking. His voice is hoarse, and he's running a slight fever. He's also having trouble breathing.

After a panicky call to the doctor you learn that these are the symptoms of croup, a common viral infection of the vocal cords that strikes babies and preschoolers mainly during the fall and spring.

Though it's often thought of as a single ailment, croup is more accurately a symptom of many different viruses, says Marjorie Hogan, M.D., an instructor of pediatrics at the University of Minnesota and a pediatrician at the Hennepin County Medical Center in Minneapolis. "It can be very frightening—to both parents and children—because the swelling in the throat that causes the barking cough can also make breathing difficult," she says. Some children with croup also experience what is called stridor, a vibrating sound that occurs when they breathe in. It's especially noticeable when they cry.

In most cases, croup can be treated successfully at home with very simple measures.

Stay calm. The reason you need to stay calm is that you want your child to stay calm. "The symptoms of croup get worse when the child gets agitated," says Dr. Hogan. "As he's gasping for more breath, he breathes faster. If you can calm him, he'll breathe slower and more air can get in and out."

Turn on the hot water. If your child is having breathing difficulties, take him into the bathroom and turn on a hot shower to get the room really steamy, suggests Dr. Hogan. "The child will be able to breathe more easily in the steam. No one is really sure why this works, but it may decrease the inflammation so the swelling goes down."

WHEN TO SEE THE DOCTOR

Sometimes those crouplike sounds can signal something far more serious: epiglottitis, an inflammation of the lidlike cartilage that covers the windpipe. You should suspect epiglottitis, says Birt Harvey, M.D., professor of pediatrics at Stanford University School of Medicine in Stanford, California, if your child is between two and six years of age and has any of the following symptoms:

• High fever.
• Forward-leaning posture when sitting.
• Drooling.
• Difficulty swallowing, with a very sore throat.

Seek immediate medical attention, so the airway can be kept open and treatment can be started immediately.

Hit the cold air. One of the curious things about croup is what happens when panicky parents bundle their child into the car for the drive to the hospital. "Suddenly, the problem stops," says Dr. Hogan. "For some reason, cold air—like steamy air—can be really beneficial." So you may be able to help your child just by opening the window (if it's a cool night) or by taking him into an air-conditioned room.

Use a humidifier. "Turn your cool-mist vaporizer up full blast," says Shirley Menard, R.N., a certified pediatric nurse practitioner and assistant professor at the University of Texas Health Science Center at San Antonio School of Nursing. "You can either let the vaporizer douse the entire room or direct it toward the child." You need to get a lot of moisture into the air before this will be effective, she says.

Some experts recommend a warm-mist vaporizer, "but I always recommend the cool mist because if the child gets out of bed and falls on it, he won't burn himself," says Loraine Stern, M.D., associate clinical professor of pediatrics at the University of California, Los Angeles, and the author of *When Do I Call the Doctor?* "Just be sure to use a vaporizer with a filter that's designed to filter out impurities, because those can aggravate breathing difficulties in an allergic child." Clean the vaporizer often, following the manufacturer's instructions.

Control the fever. "Children who have a fever tend to breathe faster to cool off their bodies, and that makes their breathing more difficult," says Dr. Stern. You can give your child acetaminophen (Children's Tylenol) to bring the fever down. Check the package directions for the correct dosage for your child's age and weight. If your child is under age two, consult a physician.

Give plenty of fluids. "We all lose some fluid from the body with each breath. But for the child breathing harder and faster with croup, this can become a real problem," says Menard. "You can give the child frequent, small sips of an over-the-counter electrolyte replacement fluid such as Pedialyte—or even Gatorade." But any clear liquid—like broth or apple juice—will help restore fluids to the child's body.

Sleep with the child. Croup is scary. For your own peace of mind, it might be best to sleep in the same room as your child, says Dr. Stern. That way you'll be right there if he experiences breathing difficulties. For some reason croup tends to get worse at night. "It may be because the body produces less of the hormone cortisone at night. There's some evidence that cortisone can help a little bit with croup," says Dr. Stern. If you can't sleep in the same room as the child, use a monitoring device that will alert you if there's any problem.

CRYING

For most parents, a crying baby is no laughing matter. Many babies cry an hour or more each day, frustrating their parents, who know that crying is a baby's only language yet are unable to translate it. When is it hunger? When is it pain? When do those plaintive wails that touch us to our very core mean "Come and pick me up"?

What most parents learn in the first three months of a newborn's life is that comforting a crying baby is a matter of trial and error. Eventually, the signals will become clear, as parents get better at guessing what baby wants. But in these early few months, a lot of crying seems to be a general plea for comfort.

Should you *always* comfort a crying baby? In general, the experts say, a baby under 12 weeks may need frequent holding and cuddling. After three months, babies should be given the opportunity to learn to comfort themselves, or crying may become a habit. Here are a few comforting techniques to try—but results are not guaranteed.

Check for physical causes. "Make certain nothing is hurting the child," says Dena Hofkosh, M.D., assistant professor of pediatrics at the University of Pittsburgh School of Medicine and coordinator of the Infant Development Program at Children's Hospital of Pittsburgh. Look for open diaper pins, scratchy clothing, a crib toy poking your baby in the tummy. Also, look for fever or other symptoms of illness, such as a rash. Did the baby burp after his last feeding? If not, he may be having gas pains.

Try a quick pick-me-up. Some babies cry just because they want to be held, and as long as the baby is under 12 weeks old, you shouldn't hesitate. "A lot of parents think they'll spoil babies if they pick them up when they cry, but that's just not the case," says Dr. Hofkosh. "A study done at McGill University found that babies who were held more cried less."

Give daily love pats. Touch your child gently and frequently even when he doesn't need it. Essentially what you are doing is providing unconditional love and rewarding noncrying behavior at the same time, says Edward Christophersen, Ph.D., clinical psychologist at Children's Mercy Hospital, professor of pediatrics at the University of Missouri–Kansas City School of Medicine, and author of *Baby Owner's Manual: What to Expect and How to Survive the First Year.*

Tune in to the Fussy Hour. Many babies have a predictable fussy period each day. Although it can occur at any hour, it often comes around dinnertime, when the whole family is home and meal preparations are under way. "Once you're convinced that's what it is, think of that crying period as an exercise time for your baby," says Robert Mendelson, M.D., a pediatrician and clinical professor of pediatrics at Oregon Health Sciences University in Portland. "It's the baby's way of jogging, burning off the excess energy he has." So you might just want to let these crying spells run their course.

Bring on the rhythm and music. "A lot of babies respond well to a recorded heartbeat," says Dr. Mendelson. There's something primal and soothing about the rhythmic thump-thump that was their piped-in sound track for nine months. Playing music can also help: Many crying babies are distracted by George Gershwin's "Rhapsody in Blue" and Raffi's "Baby Beluga." Your humming can be very soothing to a fussy child. Even a running vacuum cleaner or clothes dryer can calm him down.

Put them in motion. A walk around the house might sooth your infant. Your baby may also respond to gentle rocking, either in your arms or in a baby swing or cradle. "For very irritable babies, vertical rocking seems to work," says Dr. Hofkosh. Hold the baby on your lap or shoulder and rock up and down gently, applying some pressure to the chest and belly. "Babies like frontal pressure, which is almost like being tucked into the womb again," says Dr. Hofkosh.

Take a ride. For some babies, a drive in the car is like a tranquilizer. When one of her daughters was a baby, Dr. Hofkosh recalls, "we drove around for an hour and a half in a pouring rainstorm because I couldn't deal with the crying any more. I figured it was better than sitting home and waiting it out."

Use a baby carrier. "Some babies love the close comfort of being held on your chest in a front pack," says Dr. Hofkosh. "Some parents like the backpack, but it may be better if the baby's front is in contact with Mommy or Daddy. It's also convenient. You can get things done with the baby sleeping there. I know I ate many meals with my daughters in a front pack."

Change positions . . . but not too much. Like the rest of us, babies can get bored or uncomfortable staying in the same position, says Lottie Mendelson, R.N., a pediatric nurse practitioner in Portland, Oregon, and coauthor of *The Complete Book of Parenting*, with her husband, Robert. Some babies like to be vertical on your shoulder, while others like to peer at the world from your lap. But don't switch too frequently, says Dr. Hofkosh. "Some babies take a longer time to adapt to a particular position, so you need to avoid going quickly from one to the next." Give the baby time to figure out whether she feels okay in the new position, advises Mendelson.

Turn down the light and noise. Babies who are easily overstimulated—or those who have had a big day full of strange faces and voices and a lot of handling—may need a little time to decompress, particularly before bed, says Dr. Hofkosh. By turning down the lights and keeping voices low, you can help the overstimulated baby relax.

Don't plug cries with food. "It's very satisfying for parents who hear a baby cry to be able to do something about it, and feeding is the most primal nurturing activity we can do," says Dr. Hofkosh. But she advises against feeding as the first response to a baby's cry.

Babies do cry when they're hungry, but that's far from the only reason, notes Dr. Hofkosh. A baby who cries when she's bored will probably stop crying if you nurse or give her a bottle, but you will miss the opportunity to learn what her cries *really* mean and you'll be training her to think of eating as something you do when you're bored.

As a rule of thumb, says Dr. Hofkosh, most breastfed babies feed every 90 minutes to 2 hours and bottle-fed babies can often wait 2 to 2½ hours between feedings. "If she cries sooner than that, it makes sense to try other things before offering food again," says Dr. Hofkosh.

Take a break. It's almost impossible for parents to remain calm when they've got a crying baby on their hands. Every "wah" seems to be saying, "You're a bad parent." But you're not a bad parent if your child is crying, especially if you've done everything you can to console him," says Dr. Mendelson. "A truly fussy baby is often inconsolable, which can drive parents crazy."

Parents need to make sure they get regular breaks from a fussy baby, he suggests. Arrange to get an hour or two off daily—and possibly an entire afternoon off once a week—leaving the baby with a grandparent or trusted babysitter. And have an occasional evening out with your partner just to recharge.

Remember, this too shall pass. "Recognize that crying, especially in a challenging baby, is time-limited," explains Dr. Hofkosh. "Tell yourself that you can help your baby be okay even though he's the kind who cries all the time. Remind yourself it isn't a personality trait that's going to last forever."

Give them some time. After a baby is 12 weeks old, you can begin to change your strategy. Rushing to comfort a crying baby or child at the first peep deprives her of a wonderful learning experience, says Dr. Christophersen. If you take care of her every need, she'll never learn how to calm herself, he warns. "The only way I know to reduce crying is by teaching self-quieting skills," he says. So wait a few minutes—how long is dictated by your tolerance for crying—to see if the baby can find a way to quiet herself. If she's not in true discomfort, a baby over the age of about 12 weeks will often distract herself by playing with her feet, sucking her thumb or examining her surroundings rather than screaming for you.

Put your baby to bed awake. Bedtime is often the best time to teach babies how to self-quiet, says Dr. Christophersen. Though there's a real temptation to nurse or rock babies to sleep, parents and babies eventually pay the price of sleepless nights (and cranky next days) because the baby comes to associate nursing or rocking with falling asleep. That may be fine at 8:00 P.M., but it's not such a pleasure at 3:00 A.M. when the baby begins crying for her "sleeping pill," in the form of a long rocking session.

"If a baby nurses before bedtime and gets drowsy, carry her, maybe bounce her around a little, talk to her, change her diaper, wipe her gums and put her to bed," says Dr. Christophersen. "She may go, 'Wah, wah wah,' and then she'll be gone. Best of all, she'll learn how to put herself to sleep. And if you know your baby can self-quiet, you won't feel like you're abandoning her."

Take your baby out of the crib before he cries. "A lot of parents use their babies as a snooze alarm," says Dr. Christophersen. "After 12 weeks, many babies who once woke up crying wake up babbling. But their parents don't pick them up until they cry. That teaches the child he *has to* cry before you'll pick him up. I'd much rather have parents teach children they get picked up for babbling and cooing, not for screaming."

DAWDLING

Lisa is 3 and her mother, Katherine, is 33, but at 7:30 every morning, it's Mom who comes closest to having a tantrum. If you've ever tried to get a small child moving in a hurry, you'll empathize with Katherine's struggle. Frustration isn't a strong enough word to describe what you feel when your preschooler takes a half hour to find her shoes, or your 7-year-old can't do his homework because it takes him forever to round up a pencil and paper, or your 11-year-old makes the whole car pool wait, morning after morning, no matter how many times you've said, "Today you're leaving *on time.*"

Yet grown-up tantrums, pleading and nagging aren't the answer, agree the experts. There's usually a message behind the dawdler's molasses-like movements. Figure it out and you're halfway there. Here are some suggestions for coping.

Recognize that it may be normal. "Dawdling is a normal part of development in young children," points out Cynthia Whitham, a licensed clinical social worker and staff therapist at the University of California, Los Angeles, Parent Training Clinic and author of *Win the Whining War and Other Skirmishes:* "So sometimes you may just have to relax and accept it. The child's behavior will probably get better as she matures." But even older children may need a couple of reminders or an incentive, she notes.

Teach some clock-watching. "Preschoolers don't have much concept of time, so urging them to get ready because you have to be someplace 'on time' means very little to them," says William Womack, M.D., associate professor in the Department of Child Psychiatry at the University of Washington School of Medicine and codirector of the Stress Management Clinic of Children's Hospital and Medical Center, both in Seattle. "Once kids learn how to tell time in first or second grade, it's easier to get them to do things on time." Teaching your child to read the clock—then checking the time together—helps to make her more aware of *when* you have to get things done.

Only interrupt when you must. "No one on the planet likes to be interrupted, yet all day long we're interrupting children's play to get them to do things we want them to do," notes Whitham. When a child resists being interrupted, we mistakenly call it dawdling. Rather than interrupt suddenly, give your child a "warning" announcement, so she knows there's a change-of-activity coming up. For example, you might say, "In five minutes it will be time to turn off the TV and come to dinner."

Praise the child who shows stick-to-it-iveness. Whitham suggests parents say, "Good job!" when a child does something quickly. Praise anything the child does that is efficient and the opposite of dawdling. By the time a child is nine or ten, he understands the concept of being organized, so you can begin praising him for that. Some children respond well when you say, "Good planning!"

Use the star system. "Buy some colored stars and a calendar that contains large boxes," suggests Robert R. Butterworth, Ph.D., a Los Angeles–based clinical psychologist specializing in treating children and adolescents. Then use those stars as awards for prompt behavior, he suggests. "If your child regularly dawdles over homework, for instance, explain that from now on, for every day he does his homework promptly, he gets a star on the calendar." Agree that once he gets a certain number, he'll get a reward, suggests Dr. Butterworth.

Put on a happy face. For preschoolers who can't read yet, draw or cut out pictures of the tasks the child needs to do, suggests Whitham. Then place "happy face" stickers on a chart next to tasks that have been completed. "The positive approach works best," she notes.

Give positive attention. A child who drags his feet may actually be getting more attention from his parents for dawdling than he would for being efficient, according to Dr. Butterworth. "Attention can be either negative or positive," he says. "Children

IS YOUR CHILD TRYING TO TELL YOU SOMETHING?

If your school-age child is dawdling all the time, it may seem as though he's purposely trying to irritate you. That may be *precisely* what's happening, says William Womack, M.D., associate professor in the Department of Child Psychiatry at the University of Washington School of Medicine and codirector of the Stress Management Clinic of Children's Hospital and Medical Center, both in Seattle. "You need to think about the meaning of the dawdling behavior. Does your child dislike the activity that's being postponed? He could be trying to say to you, 'The rest of my life is unpleasant so I'm going to make you pay by holding back now.'

"We make lots of decisions *for* our children," notes Dr. Womack, "and as a result, they may feel helpless. If there are frequent tests of will between you and your child, take a look at whether he is able to make decisions in other areas of his life. If he has decided that a particular elective activity is not his cup of tea, it might be best to allow him to drop it rather than force him to continue when he insists on dawdling."

don't look at the type of attention they get, but rather at its intensity." In other words, if you say, 'Oh, you came on time,' that's only a three on the attention scale (even though it's positive). But if you yell, 'I'm tired of you always being late,' that's an eight on the attention scale (even though it's negative). "That's why it's so important to give lots of positive attention," says Dr. Butterworth.

Make it clear. "Find out if your child is having trouble understanding what he's supposed to do," says Dr. Butterworth. "Make your expectations crystal clear." With an older child, you can sit down and actually write out a schedule of the week. "That way, both you and the child know exactly when things need to be accomplished," he says.

Give one command at a time. Preschoolers can respond to only one command at a time, says Whitham. "Don't surround your requests by a huge paragraph. Make a short, clear statement ending in a period, such as 'Go get your shoes. Then come back to me, and I'll tell you the next thing.'"

Make eye contact. Some children become "immune" to long-distance commands shouted at them by a far-away parent. Whitham suggests first calling your child to come to you—or going over to your child—rather than yelling a command across the house. Then look directly into her eyes when making your request.

Discuss the upcoming events. Ask a school-age child, "What's your plan? You have that TV program you enjoy watching and you have this homework assignment. How do you plan to fit everything in?" According to Whitham, this helps the child take responsibility, and she'll be more motivated to get a task done so she can move on to things she enjoys.

Get ready . . . get set . . . get out the stopwatch. "Little children get a big kick out of being timed or racing with you," says Whitham. When you need your child to get moving quickly, say, "I'll time you," or "Let's see how fast you can go." Use a stopwatch or the second hand of a watch. Be sure to praise success with comments like, "Wow, ten seconds—was that fast!" As a last resort, use timing in this way: "I'm going to count to three, and I want you to run and get your shoes."

DIAPER RASH

Cloth . . . or disposable? It's the first, critical decision that parents make about their newborn's immediate future.

But whichever diaper you choose, the goal is the same—to keep your baby's bottom as dry as possible through those incontinent first years of life. Succeed in that, and your infant has a pretty good chance of avoiding that ruby-red bane of babies' buns—diaper rash.

Fortunately, diaper rash is rarely serious. But just try telling that to your uncomfortable infant who's wiggling, kicking and complaining with a preverbal vigor that keeps you hopping. You're sure to lose some sleep before it's over—but luckily, prompt action and a few preventive steps can usually take care of that rash. Here's where to start.

Change frequently. "Paper or cloth diapers work equally well as long as you change them whenever they're wet or soiled," says Sam Solis, M.D., chairman of the Department of Pediatrics at Children's Hospital in New Orleans, assistant professor of pediatrics at Tulane University School of Medicine and a pediatrician in Metairie, Louisiana. At home, that's easy enough to do. But be sure to carry enough diapers when you're traveling as well.

Rinse cloth diapers with vinegar. If you have reusable cloth diapers, rinse them in vinegar during the wash to change the pH and help reduce diaper rash. "Just add ¼ cup of plain white kitchen vinegar to each load of diapers during the final rinse cycle of your wash," suggests Becky Luttkus, head instructor at the National Academy of Nannies in Denver. Also, don't use fabric softeners when washing diapers, because the softeners put a coating on the diapers that keeps them from absorbing as well, adds Luttkus.

Abolish plastic pants. If your baby is in cloth diapers, don't cover them with plastic pants except when you absolutely have to. "Plastic pants keep the moisture in, which is just what you don't want," says Dr. Solis. "Moisture can cause or worsen diaper rash." He recommends thick cloth diaper covers as a better alternative, since they allow the skin to breathe.

Go natural. If you change your tot frequently enough, she might not need any powder at all. But if you do need a baby powder, use plain cornstarch, recommends Daniel Bronfin, M.D., staff pediatrician at the Ochsner Clinic and assistant clinical professor of pediatrics at Tulane University School of Medicine in New Orleans.

"A lot of people, particularly grandparents, enjoy applying powders and baby lotion after a diaper change, but these won't prevent diaper rash," says Dr. Bronfin. "In fact, because these products usually contain perfume and additives, they may even *cause* a rash."

Wipe out wipes. In an ideal world, a baby's bottom would be cleaned with mild soap and water and rinsed well with every diaper change. But most parents use wipes that may contain alcohol, perfume and soap that remain on the skin, notes Lynn Sugarman, M.D., a pediatrician with Tenafly Pediatrics in Tenafly, New Jersey, and an associate in clinical pediatrics at Babies Hospital, Columbia Presbyterian Medical Center in New York City. "Wipes can be irritating to the skin, especially when your baby has a diaper rash. At the first sign of a rash, switch to soap and water," says Dr. Sugarman.

Use a spray bottle. Dr. Bronfin recommends removing stool with warm water mixed with a drop or two of baby oil. "Use a spray bottle to spray the mixture on the diaper area, then wipe it off with a clean cloth," he suggests. This method will be less irritating to your baby.

Air it out. The diaper rash will heal faster if you let air get to the area. "Try to let your baby go without a diaper for 10 to 15 minutes after each diaper change," suggests Dr. Solis.

Try a sitz bath. When a rash is really uncomfortable, a sitz bath helps restore moisture to the skin and speeds healing, says Dr. Solis. "Two or three times a day, fill the tub with a few inches of warm water and let your child sit in the tub and play with his toys. You only have to do it for five to ten minutes each time, but it really makes a difference," he says.

Create a barrier. Protect irritated skin from further contact with waste by applying a thick layer of an over-the-counter barrier cream such as Balmex ointment or A and D Ointment, suggests Dr. Sugarman.

Snip some elastic. If your child is outfitted in disposable diapers, there's some custom tailoring you can do to get the air circulating a bit better, according to Dr. Bronfin. Put the diapers on as loosely as possible, rather than snug at the waist. Also, snip some of the elastic from the bands around the leg openings, he suggests. And make sure you choose a diaper size that is roomy enough to allow for some air space.

EAR INFECTIONS

If your child gets through her toddler years without an ear infection, her guardian angel must be working overtime.

"A middle ear infection, also known as otitis media, is one of the most frequently diagnosed childhood illnesses," says Michael Macknin, M.D., head of the Section of General Pediatrics at the Cleveland Clinic Foundation in Ohio, clinical professor at Pennsylvania State University Medical School in Hershey and associate professor of pediatrics at Ohio State University Medical School in Columbus. The root of the problem lies in the eustachian tubes, narrow passageways which connect the back of the nose and throat to the middle ear. When a eustachian tube functions properly, it allows air into the middle ear while keeping out bacteria and debris from the nose and mouth. It also permits any fluid that may collect to drain out.

Babies and young children, however, have very tiny eustachian tubes that tend to get swollen and blocked each time a cold, sinus infection or allergy attack comes along. A swollen eustachian tube can't do its job, says Dr. Macknin, and that makes your child more susceptible to middle ear infection.

Although your child should outgrow the tendency to get ear infections, lots of kids suffer with them throughout their preschool years. While you can't prevent ear infections completely, doctors say there are a number of ways you can reduce your child's chances of getting an infection. And even if your child gets one, you can make him more comfortable. Here are some suggestions.

Use a painkiller for short-term relief. Prescription antibiotics should provide pain relief within 12 to 24 hours. But while you wait for that relief to kick in, your child can take acetaminophen (Children's Tylenol) if he needs it, says Charles D. Bluestone, M.D., professor of otolaryngology at the University of Pittsburgh School of Medicine and director of the Department of Pediatric Otolaryngology and the Otitis Media Research Center at the Children's Hospital of Pittsburgh. Check the package directions for the correct dosage for your child's age and weight. If your child is under age two, consult a physician.

Don't rely on over-the-counter ear drops that contain a local anesthetic to relieve the pain. "None of them have been shown to be effective in controlled trials," Dr. Bluestone says.

Try some "warm-up exercises." Children with ear pain may find warmth soothing. "I sometimes recommend that parents put two or three drops of warm mineral oil into their child's ear," says Gerald Zahtz, M.D., an assistant professor of otolaryngology at Albert Einstein College of Medicine in New York City and physician at Long Island Jewish Medical Center in New Hyde Park, New York. "But it's critical that the drops be the correct temperature. If they are too warm or too cold, you may induce dizziness. So aim for body temperature."

Hold the mineral oil bottle in your hand for about 15 minutes before you put in the drops. Or fill a large bowl with hot water and keep the bottle in the water for about 5 minutes. Test the oil against your skin before putting it in the ear.

Caution: Never use drops if the ear is draining, says Dr. Zahtz.

Use a warm-water bottle. Dr. Zahtz recommends holding a hot-water bottle against the ear, but it should be filled with warm, *not* hot, water, he says. Also, wrap the bottle in a towel before placing it against the ear.

Don't smoke around your child. Studies show that the children of smokers have more colds and ear infections than children of nonsmokers. "If you smoke, the best thing you can do for your child is to quit. But if you don't quit, at least smoke outside. Don't smoke around your child," Dr. Macknin says.

Breastfeed your baby. Breastfeeding provides a protective benefit, because antibodies passed along in the breast milk may decrease your baby's chance of getting an infection, notes Dr. Bluestone. There also seems to be something in mother's milk that helps prevent bacteria from sticking to the mucous membrane of the throat, making it less likely that germs will travel up the eustachian tube into the ear, he says. "If you want to help prevent ear infections, you should breastfeed your baby for at least the first six months," Dr. Bluestone advises.

Feed baby in an upright position. When you bottle-feed or nurse your baby, keep his body in an upright position, especially if he tends to regurgitate a bit of his meal. "If your baby is in a horizontal position while feeding, regurgitated milk can pass into the eustachian tube, and possibly cause an infection," says Dr. Zahtz. This is less likely to happen if you hold your baby at an angle of 45 degrees or more while feeding, he says.

Ask the doctor about milk allergy. In rare cases, recurrent ear infections may be due to milk allergy, says Dr. Zahtz. "If a child with chronic infections is less than a year old, I try taking him off all milk products for four weeks to see what develops." Don't make any diet changes without talking to your doctor first, though, advises Dr. Zahtz, or you could seriously compromise your child's health.

Watch for early signs of sinus infection. If your child has a cold, and the nasal mucus starts to thicken and become colored, consult a doctor. Thick yellow or green mucus may indicate a sinus infection that needs to be treated with antibiotics, says Dr. Zahtz. If the problem is treated early, there is a good chance that it won't lead to an ear infection, he says.

EATING PROBLEMS

E ating is one area where kids can begin to control their parents. Mom and Dad—worried that their slender, picky eater isn't getting enough nourishment—resort to threatening, bribing, cajoling or catering to their child to try to get him to eat.

Once an eating problem develops, it takes patience and time to deal with it. Here are some hints from the experts to help you over the hurdle.

Assess your expectations. If your child eats small portions, don't worry. Some children don't need large amounts of food, says Alvin N. Eden, M.D., associate clinical professor of pediatrics at New York Hospital–Cornell Medical Center, chairman of the Department of Pediatrics at Wyckoff Heights Medical Center, both in New York City, and author of *Positive Parenting* and *Dr. Eden's Healthy Kids*. Also realize that children can vary a lot in their day-to-day intake. They may be ravenous one day and pick at their food the next.

Serve small portions. "Put less food on your child's plate than you think he'll eat," says Quentin Van Meter, M.D., a pediatrician and associate professor of clinical pediatrics at Emory University School of Medicine in Atlanta. "Piles of food on a plate can turn off a child's appetite."

The appropriate portion size for kids is surprisingly small—and you can always serve seconds, if the child wants more, points out Dr. Eden.

Snacks are fine—but keep them small. Your child may be turning up her nose at her nutritious dinner because her tummy is full of the bag of chips she had after school. Don't deprive her of the after-school snack—but these snacks have to be small if you expect your child to eat a full dinner, says Barton D. Schmitt, M.D., professor of pediatrics at the University of Colorado School of Medicine, director of consultative services at the

Ambulatory Care Center at Children's Hospital of Denver, and author of *Your Child's Health.*

Limit the drinks, too. Many parents underestimate how filling juice and milk can be, says Dr. Van Meter. He recommends limiting juice to 6 ounces a day and milk to 16 ounces.

"The fats and sugars in these fluids can curb the appetite just enough to keep your child active and happy, but he won't be getting a balanced meal," he says. Soda pop is even worse, because it fills up the child without supplying any essential nutrients.

Consider mini-meals. Some busy, active children function better on small meals throughout the day, says Corinne Montandon, Dr.P.H., R.D., assistant professor of nutrition at Baylor College of Medicine and the Children's Nutrition Research Center, both in Houston. Toddlers, in particular, may need nutritious small meals about two to three hours apart. This doesn't mean that Mom has to prepare meals on demand, however. Keep a supply of healthy snack foods on hand. "Give your child some cheese and fruit, or graham crackers and a small glass of milk," suggests Dr. Montandon. Then don't expect your child to eat a big meal at dinner.

Plan ahead. "Children who must wait too long between meals get so hungry that they get cranky," says Dr. Montandon, "and cranky kids do not eat well." If you know that your child gets famished because you can't get dinner on the table before 7:00 P.M., furnish a nourishing mini-meal earlier, or cook dinner ahead of time so you can serve it earlier.

Involve your child. Decide together what you are going to serve, advises Dr. Montandon. Offer nutritious choices and then let your child pick. "Children who are given the chance to make food decisions are more likely to eat what they choose," she says.

Let your child feed herself. When a child is pushing her food around the plate, it's tempting to pick up the spoon and try

DON'T WORRY—IT'S NORMAL

Suddenly it seems that your child is devouring an enormous amount of food at each meal, and you're worried that he's overeating.

But your child may simply be going through a growth spurt, explains Alvin N. Eden, M.D., associate clinical professor of pediatrics at the New York Hospital–Cornell Medical Center, chairman of the Department of Pediatrics at Wyckoff Heights Medical Center, both in New York City, and author of *Positive Parenting* and *Dr. Eden's Healthy Kids*. While in a growth phase, children may consume large quantities of food to keep up with the calories being burned. Just be sure that your child is eating a variety of foods and isn't loading up mostly on sweets or fatty foods.

If you're concerned, check with your pediatrician. Your child's pediatrician plots your child's weight and height on a special chart. If the child's growth deviates markedly from his usual patterns, that will signal that something is wrong.

Otherwise, relax—and keep plenty of healthy foods on hand for your hungry, growing child.

to tease her into eating, says Dr. Schmitt. Don't do it. "Once your child is old enough to use a spoon by herself [usually 15 to 16 months of age], never again pick it up for her," he says. "If your child is hungry, she will feed herself."

Refrain from forcing. Just about the worst thing you can do is force your child to eat, agree experts. This will frustrate you, make your child resentful and create a power struggle that no one will win—and it won't solve the problem, says Dr. Schmitt. "How much a child chooses to eat is governed by the appetite center in the brain," he explains. "If you try to control how much your child eats, he will rebel. Trust the appetite center."

Keep mealtimes pleasant. This is what you should concentrate on, rather than what your child does or doesn't eat, says Dr. Schmitt. "Draw your children into the conversation, and don't make mealtimes a time for criticism or arguments," he advises.

Forget about forcing your child to stay at the table with his food after the rest of the family has left. "This only develops unpleasant associations with mealtimes," says Dr. Schmitt.

Insist on politeness. Let your child know that he is expected to be at the table on time, sit with the family while they eat and refrain from making faces and rude comments about the food, suggests Dr. Eden.

Never nag—or praise. Keep eating as matter-of-fact as possible, says Dr. Schmitt. Don't fuss at your problem eater for not finishing her food, or praise her when she does. You want your child to eat to satisfy her appetite, not to please you. And never discuss how much or how little your child eats when you're in her presence.

Don't cook on demand. Never get up and make special meals for a picky eater, says Dr. Eden. Serve a well-balanced meal and let your child eat what she wants from what you have served.

Eliminate "gag" foods. Some kids have a natural aversion to foods that they associate with being sick. If a child happened to become ill after a certain food, that food may turn his stomach. Rather than force him to eat those foods, parents should avoid serving them, advises Dr. Schmidt. "Those foods should be put in a special category and simply eliminated from the menu," he says.

Avoid the dessert dilemma. This is a classic Catch-22. If everyone digs into a rich gooey cake for dessert but the noneater isn't allowed any, you're reinforcing the idea that "good" food is a reward for eating "bad" food. If you do give cake to the problem eater, you're letting her fill up on empty calories, explains Dr. Van Meter.

Your best bet is to serve nutritious desserts that are considered part of the meal: fruit, gelatin with fruit or yogurt, he suggests.

Ease your mind with vitamins. If you're worried about your child's intake of certain nutrients, ask your pediatrician about giving your child a daily vitamin and mineral supplement, says Dr. Van Meter. The supplement may not be necessary, but it can put your mind at ease.

Get expert advice. When a child is thin, it's often because he's quite active or just naturally slender. But it can also be something more serious, says Dr. Schmitt. Some illnesses, such as infestation with roundworms, can cause unnatural thinness. And pre-teens—girls especially—can develop a serious eating disorder called anorexia nervosa.

Call your physician if you notice that your child is losing weight, gags on or vomits some foods or has any other symptoms of illness, such as fever or diarrhea.

FEARS

The bogeyman. Monsters under the bed. Animal attacks. Being kidnapped. AIDS. At one time or another, your child may be beset by fears such as these.

"As a parent, you should understand that all these fears are normal, but how you react to them can determine whether fears go away, stay around or get worse," says Sheila Ribordy, Ph.D., a clinical psychologist specializing in children and families and professor of psychology and director of clinical training in the Department of Psychology at De Paul University in Chicago.

Children may have different fears at different developmental stages. It's not unusual for a child who's been sleeping calmly in a dark room to suddenly, at age five, begin begging for a night-light to keep monsters at bay. "Common fears among younger children are of imaginary things, like the bogeyman," says Dr. Ribordy. "In spite of our protestations that there aren't any monsters and ghosts, until they're well into school age, children have a capacity to believe there are.

"Older children, on the other hand, often become afraid of things they hear about on TV: environmental contamination, AIDS, kidnappings, abuse. These messages are overwhelming to them emotionally," says Dr. Ribordy.

While at times it may seem like a scary world even to adults, it is possible to make it a little less scary for children by following these suggestions.

Help them use their imagination. It's imagination that makes kids picture monsters lurking in the dark or believe that a real, live animal or bug will suddenly attack them. But they can also use their imaginations to beat those fears, says Thomas Olkowski, Ph.D., a clinical psychologist in private practice in Denver.

"Have a child imagine something she's afraid of, such as a dark room or a dog, and then visualize herself entering the dark room or approaching the dog without anything awful happening. She should practice a number of times until she finally feels comfortable," Dr. Olkowski suggests.

This can also work with older children whose fears might be based on more realistic concerns such as going to a dance, transferring to a new school or performing in the class play. Imagining themselves going through the steps is something like a rehearsal, he says, and gives them confidence when the real thing comes along.

Get real. After the child has practiced approaching his worst fears in his imagination, help him do it in real life, but in small steps, says Dr. Olkowski. "Set up situations in which the child feels absolutely in control. If the child is afraid of animals, for example, go to a pet shop, but just look through the window at first."

Read all about it. Nothing is better than information to help banish fears, both real and imaginary. "If a child is afraid of spiders and insects, for instance, he can read about them in a book," says Dr. Olkowski. Dr. Ribordy gave one young boy who was terrified of lightning a therapeutic homework assignment: "I sent him to the library to research lightning, as part of a science project. Learning about the phenomenon of lightning has desensitized him. Now he thinks about it in a different way. It's not an ominous, scary thing."

Offer reassurance. Kids need to be told that they have little to fear from what they fear. This is especially true for older children, says Dr. Ribordy. "They have very real fears about illness and death. They think, 'What would happen if I lost my Mom? What if I get AIDS?'"

When a child expresses such fears, you can respond by explaining just how low the probability is of any of those things actually happening to him, she says. "It also helps to assure your child that it's your job, not his, to worry about such things," according to Dr. Ribordy.

Arm that child with a flashlight. Bedtime may be the time when your child's fears manifest themselves. That's when the hideous creatures of the night supposedly come to terrorize small, defenseless children in their beds. So you need to make your child less defenseless, says Dr. Ribordy.

She recommends giving a child her own flashlight. "To a child who is afraid of the dark, this symbolizes control," she observes. Even if the child doesn't use it, she knows the flashlight is always next to her bed and she can switch it on any time.

Fight monsters with a little magic. Sometimes it helps if you can empower the child in a special way. Barbara Howard, M.D., assistant clinical professor of pediatrics at Duke University Medical Center in Durham, North Carolina, advocates "monster spray"—a spray bottle containing a harmless substance, like water—for the parent to use at bedtime as a preventive measure to keep any imaginary creatures at bay. "You can use it once or as often as needed to reassure the child," says Dr. Howard.

"I've been criticized for suggesting this, because if you're preparing to 'exorcise' the monsters, doesn't that mean you're saying there actually *are* monsters? Logically speaking, you shouldn't do it," she says. "But, in fact, it works, because the child thinks the parent is all-powerful and accepts the spray as a potent weapon."

Deputize teddy. "Ask the child to pick out a teddy bear or other stuffed animal he feels good about to be his protector," suggests Dr. Olkowski. "This also gives the child a sense of control over the things he fears, whether they're real or not."

Monitor TV viewing. "Be very careful about what your children are watching," says Dr. Howard. "There are a lot of scary things on TV." Sitcoms may be fine—but you certainly don't want a fearful child to watch shows that involve bloodshed, intimidation or violence.

Use relaxation exercises. Taking deep breaths or imagining a quiet, safe place can help a child relax and feel less fearful, says Dr. Howard. "Children are actually better at using these methods than adults. Have your child lie still and imagine herself drifting on a cloud or lying on the beach—something that would be relaxing and fun."

Set limits. Often, says Dr. Howard, those monsters kids are afraid of are *themselves*. "Nighttime fears especially are symbolic of things going on in their lives. If children's behavior is out of control during the day, they may feel they need protection from monsters at night," she says. "What they need is better structure in their lives and more discipline, by which I mean protection from their own aggression. If they're allowed to hit or to run rampant over their parents, who are supposed to be all-powerful, they're likely to have nighttime fears." By taking back control, you can help put those fears at rest.

Tell special bedtime stories. Since most kids are afraid of things they can't control, you should tell bedtime stories about characters who accomplished difficult tasks or overcame their fears, says Dr. Howard. "Tell stories of how someone mastered things he was afraid of or did something he didn't think he could do. You can tell stories from your own childhood, or read from a book, such as *The Little Engine That Could*."

Have a plan. "Children are reassured by having a plan," says Dr. Ribordy. "For example, we went through a period with my son when he was afraid the house would catch on fire. So we went out and bought a fire escape ladder, and every day for a week we practiced how he would escape in case of fire. He found that very reassuring, and his fear completely went away."

FEVER

Her pajamas are rumpled, her face flushed and the tendrils of hair on her forehead are damp from sweat. When your child seems feverish, your first instinct is probably to try to cool her off. But a warm child may not necessarily be running a temperature, and even if she is, lowering the fever isn't always the best solution, says A. Gayden Robert, M.D., a pediatrician and head of general pediatrics at the Ochsner Clinic in New Orleans.

Any concerned parent will call the doctor as soon as fever starts to escalate—and with good reason. It's important to find out what's *causing* the fever. But that doesn't mean you have to bring the fever down right away.

"The fever is a symptom, not an illness," says Dr. Robert, noting that fever is often caused by a viral or bacterial infection, such as the measles or flu. "It's a defense mechanism that helps a child fight the infection."

Most doctors agree, however, that you may need to treat a fever so your child can rest more easily. If your child is crying or irritable from the fever, you'll definitely want to lower it enough to make him more comfortable, says Carol Kilmon, Ph.D., R.N., a certified pediatric nurse practitioner and assistant professor at the School of Nursing at the University of Texas Medical Branch in Galveston.

So here's how to deal with high temperature to bring your child back to the comfort zone.

TAKING THE TEMPERATURE

Time it right. The body's temperature fluctuates throughout the day, points out Sanford Kimmel, M.D., pediatrician and associate professor of clinical family medicine at the Medical College of Ohio in Toledo. It's generally highest in the late afternoon or early evening, and lowest in the morning. It can also be affected by exercise or hot foods. To get the most accurate reading, you should take your child's temperature 30 minutes after he has quieted down or 30 minutes after he's had a hot meal or drink, advises Dr. Kimmel.

Take the right approach. A baby's temperature is most accurately measured with a rectal thermometer which is shorter and has a thicker bulb than an oral thermometer, says Dr. Kimmel. Grease it with petroleum jelly, then insert the thermometer slowly no farther than 1½ inches, and hold it gently in place for at least three minutes. To do this you can put the baby on the dressing table or in your lap in the diaper-changing position, and lift the baby's legs for easy access. Or you may prefer to lay the child stomach down across the lap, spread the buttocks and then insert the thermometer.

Switch to oral. When a child is four or five, he'll usually be able to cooperate in holding an oral thermometer under his tongue for at least four minutes, says Dr. Kimmel. Digital thermometers are fast, accurate and a little safer than traditional glass mercury thermometers, but they are also more expensive. Regardless of the type of thermometer used, make sure your child sits quietly, since any activity will raise the temperature.

Assess the readout. Although 98.6° has long been considered the classic "normal" oral temperature, some people routinely have a higher temperature—so your child could have a slightly higher reading and still be perfectly normal. Your child has a fever if his temperature is more than 100.4° measured rectally, 99° under the arm, or 100° measured orally, says Dr. Robert.

LOWERING THE FEVER

Give acetaminophen. Pediatric acetaminophen will help bring the fever down, says Beth W. Hapke, M.D., a pediatrician in private practice in Fairfield, Connecticut. These products come in liquid form for infants and toddlers and chewable tablets for older children. Check the package directions for the correct dosage for your child's age and weight. If your child is under age two, consult a physician.

Doctors caution that you should *never* give your feverish child aspirin, however, as it has been linked to a serious ailment called Reye's syndrome.

Try a sponge bath. Give your child a lukewarm sponge bath for 15 to 20 minutes, says Lynn Sugarman, M.D., a pediatrician with Tenafly Pediatrics in Tenafly, New Jersey, and an associate in clinical pediatrics at Babies Hospital, Columbia Presbyterian Medical Center in New York City.

Put your child into a tub with tepid water, and sponge the water over her arms, legs and body. "As the water evaporates, it cools the body, which helps bring down the fever," Dr. Sugarman explains.

Don't use water so cold that the child shivers. Shivering will actually raise the body temperature, defeating the whole purpose of the sponge bath.

If you don't want to take your child out of bed to bathe her, you can just loosen her clothing and sponge her from a basin.

Leave the alcohol on the shelf. Parents once rubbed down feverish children with rubbing alcohol, but doctors today discourage this practice. "Besides causing shivering, alcohol can be absorbed through the skin and cause a toxic reaction in your child," says Dr. Robert. And breathing the fumes can irritate your child as well.

Supply lots of fluids. A child with a fever breathes faster than usual, which makes him lose extra fluid. If he has diarrhea, even more fluid is lost. "So make sure your child sips some liquid—whatever his stomach will tolerate," advises Dr. Kilmon. "Make the drink cool, not hot, and give frequent, small amounts rather than trying to get lots down at once."

Any beverage kids will drink is fine, as long as you steer clear of colas, tea or coffee (these are diuretics that encourage fluid loss). And you can add some variation by supplying soup, a Popsicle or gelatin.

For nursing infants, regular feedings will provide enough liquid. If your infant has had diarrhea more than 24 hours, ask your doctor about giving him Pedialyte, an oral electrolyte solution available at drugstores, suggests Dr. Kimmel.

Keep clothing light. A child in flannel PJs or bundled in a quilt will overheat quickly, making the fever worse. "Keep your child lightly dressed, and have her sleep under a thin blanket or sheet," advises Dr. Sugarman.

Make meals optional. If your feverish child doesn't want to eat, don't urge her, says Dr. Kimmel. On the other hand, if she asks for pizza, that's okay, too. "If your child is in the mood to eat a certain food, it's probably okay to give it to her," he says.

A child who has had a stomach virus or upset stomach, however, will likely prefer something simple such as toast or crackers with some jelly. Other "comfort foods" such as oatmeal and mashed potatoes as well as bananas and pudding are also good choices, says Dr. Kimmel. Avoid fruit juices, however, as these can contribute to diarrhea.

Don't expect normal. Neither acetaminophen nor sponge baths will bring your feverish child's temperature down to normal, says Daniel Bronfin, M.D., a staff pediatrician at Ochsner Clinic and assistant clinical professor in pediatrics at Tulane University School of Medicine in New Orleans. "If the fever was 104°," he says, "you may be able to get it down to 101°."

Keep your child home. As long as your child has a fever, it's best to keep him home. "The rule of thumb here is that a child can return to school after his temperature has been normal for 24 hours," says Dr. Robert. "Although we don't know for sure, we believe if the fever is gone, then the infectious risk is, too."

GROWING PAINS

Sometime between the ages of four and nine, your child may experience what are commonly called "growing pains." These mysterious pains occur in the legs—often at night—and may last for anywhere from minutes to hours and then disappear. These episodes usually occur several times per week and may continue for a year or more.

You might be surprised to learn that growing pains have nothing to do with growth. "Actually, a better name for the condition is simply limb pains of childhood," says Bram H. Bernstein, M.D., professor of clinical pediatrics at the University of Southern California and head of rheumatology at Children's Hospital of Los Angeles.

But doctors still don't have all the answers about growing pains. "In some children the pains seem to be located in the muscles, while other children get pains in the bones," notes Dr. Bernstein.

In many cases, growing pains may be nothing more than muscle soreness caused by overexertion of tight muscles. "It's similar to how you or I might feel tomorrow if we climbed a mountain today," says Dr. Bernstein. "A lot of these children are quite active. The tight muscles don't hurt when they're doing things, but do begin to hurt when they relax at night. In other patients, though, we really never know the cause."

There are a few simple remedies for growing pains. "But it's hard to predict which ones will be effective in any given case," he says. "Once your doctor has ruled out anything serious, like arthritis, you may need to try a number of remedies to find out what works for your child."

Reassure with calming words. Pain is scary to children, even if the cause is simply muscle strain, Dr. Bernstein notes. "Explain to your child that the leg pains are probably caused by overexertion and that they will soon pass. Reassurance is the most important thing. Kids need to know that what they're experiencing is not the result of any terrible disease."

Fight the pain with a pain medicine. "A mild analgesic such as acetaminophen may be all the child needs," says Dr. Bernstein. Check the package directions for the correct dosage for your child's age and weight, or check with your physician. If a mild medicine doesn't work, he says, ask your doctor about ibuprofen, an anti-inflammatory drug, which is available for young children only by prescription. "Ibuprofen seems to work better than acetaminophen in many cases, though it's not clear why," he says.

Try a hands-on approach. "Growing pains respond very well to 'mother's massage,'" says Russell Steele, M.D., professor and vice chairman of the Department of Pediatrics at Louisiana State University School of Medicine in New Orleans. "Gently massage the child's legs in the area where the pain is located until he starts to feel better."

Warm up the sore spots. Heat may be soothing, particularly if the child's pains are due to muscle soreness, says Shirley Menard, R.N., a certified pediatric nurse practitioner and assistant professor at the University of Texas Health Science Center at San Antonio School of Nursing. "A warm bath or shower, or even a heating pad, can often bring relief," she notes.

Twenty minutes in a warm bath or under a heating pad is often all that's needed, adds Dr. Bernstein. However, don't leave your child unattended with a heating pad for an extended period because he might get *too* warm.

"Go camping" in the bedroom. As a preventive measure to stop future pain episodes, it may be helpful to keep your child's legs warm at night while he's sleeping. "You don't want him to sleep all night under a heating pad or an electric blanket, because that could be dangerous," says Dr. Bernstein. "But small children can be safely bundled up in a sleeping bag. The sleeping bag will keep your child's legs warm, and he'll probably enjoy it."

IMPETIGO

If your child has a cut, a skinned knee or a scratched-open mosquito bite, she may be putting out the welcome mat for a decidedly unpleasant visitor: impetigo. This contagious bacterial skin infection occurs when strep or staph bacteria gain entry into your child's skin. A frequent site for impetigo is around the nose and mouth, but it may appear anywhere on the body.

If impetigo is caused by staph bacteria, you'll see small, fluid-filled blisters that break easily and scab over into a honey-colored crust. If strep is the culprit (and yes, that's the same strep responsible for strep throat infections), there may not be blisters, but you will see crusting.

Impetigo remains contagious, spreading to other parts of the body and even to other family members, until it is treated with an antibiotic. Small areas can be cleared up by applying an antibiotic ointment available by prescription, but a large outbreak of impetigo needs to be treated with oral antibiotics. The antibiotics do a great job of stopping the infection, but your child may still be contagious for the first two or three days of treatment. During that time, she should avoid close contact with other kids, and you should make a special effort to keep her towel and washcloth separate from everyone else's.

To help speed your child's recovery and to prevent a repeat infection, try these simple suggestions.

Keep it clean. "Wash the affected area with antibacterial soap three times a day," says Luisa Castiglia, M.D., a pediatrician in private practice in Mineola, New York.

Open it up. "If you keep the area covered up with a bandage or dressing, you may be encouraging more bacteria to grow. It's a better idea to leave the affected area exposed to the air. If your child is going out to play, you can cover it up temporarily," says Dr. Castiglia.

Encourage good hygiene. "Impetigo is often spread by scratching, so teach kids to wash their hands with soap and to keep their nails clean and short," says Fran E. Adler, M.D., a pediatrician in private practice in Upper Montclair, New Jersey.

Keep it cool. "Studies show that heat tends to increase itching, so keep your child comfortable with tepid baths," says Daniel Bronfin, M.D., staff pediatrician at the Ochsner Clinic and assistant clinical professor of pediatrics at Tulane University School of Medicine in New Orleans. The bath should be just about body temperature, not warmer. "In the summertime, it also helps to run the air conditioner," he adds.

Use a bit of antihistamine. If your child is very itchy, Benadryl can be a big help, says Dr. Bronfin. Be sure to read package directions to make certain the product is recommended for your child's age. For the correct dosage, follow package directions or consult your physician. Some doctors don't advise Benadryl cream or spray because it could cause a reaction.

Catch it early. "An infection usually won't lead to impetigo if you catch it early. At the very first sign of any infection, wash the area well and apply an over-the-counter antibacterial ointment containing bacitracin. If the infection doesn't improve or if it starts to spread, see your doctor," says Dr. Adler.

Treat diaper rash seriously. "Impetigo can develop in a diaper area if your child's rash is not cleaned and protected," says Dr. Castiglia. One of the best ways to prevent impetigo in infants is to guard against diaper rash.

Lubricate a sore nose. Impetigo is very common when a child has a runny nose, especially in the wintertime, says Dr. Adler. "A child's nose gets sore and chapped from all the rubbing and moisture, so keep the area lubricated with Vaseline so that the skin won't break down. Also, make sure that your child keeps her hands and face clean," says Dr. Adler.

LAZY EYE

L ately you've noticed that your child's right eye has been straying, looking off to the side while the other eye remains straight. In a newborn, it's common to see the eyes wander. But as a child gets older, his eyes should start focusing and work together—certainly before four months of age. So what's going on here?

A child with an eye that wanders may have amblyopia, or "lazy eye," a fairly common vision problem that may affect as many as 3 out of every 100 people, says Robert D. Gross, M.D., clinical assistant professor of pediatric ophthalmology at the University of Texas Southwestern Medical School in Dallas and a pediatric ophthalmologist at the Cook–Fort Worth Children's Medical Center in Fort Worth. While you may be concerned about what your child looks like when his eye drifts, there's much more to it than that. An amblyopic eye is actually a weak eye that has not developed normal vision, says Dr. Gross.

Amblyopia must be diagnosed by an eye doctor. Experts say early treatment by an eye specialist is critical.

To treat amblyopia, eye doctors often use a method called occlusion. By wearing a patch over the strong eye for a certain amount of time each day, the child learns to rely more on the weak eye. "The earlier you patch, the better," says Dr. Gross. "Parents may be unhappy patching a child at age two, but it may be more challenging to get the child to comply at age six. And besides, the older the child becomes, the harder it is to make a positive change in visual acuity."

Patching must be done under a doctor's supervision, and the instructions need to be followed to the letter. If your doctor recommends patching, here's how to make it easier.

Help your child see the light. "Wearing a patch isn't much fun, but you can encourage your child by actively showing him why it's necessary," says Robert B. Sanet, O.D., a developmental optometrist and director of the San Diego Center for Vision Care in Lemon Grove, California, and associate professor at

Southern California College of Optometry in Fullerton. "If your child is old enough to understand, cover his straight eye with your hand and ask him how it feels to see with the other eye. Explain that the eye is weak and that patching will make it as strong as the other eye."

Pick a patch time. Mark off a designated time for your child to wear the patch. "Call it patch time and make it the same time every day," says Dr. Gross. "That way, patching will become routine, and the child will know what to expect. If he needs to wear the patch for three hours a day, then he should get to pick which three hours."

Try to keep it on the home front. It may help to have patch time be during part of the day when the child is home. "Encourage him to pick a time period like 3:00 to 6:00 P.M., when he's not at school or day care," says Dr. Gross. He'll be less self-conscious, and therefore more willing to wear the patch if he doesn't have to wear it in front of all his classmates, he points out.

Another important reason to patch at home is that you as a parent can supervise the patching process. "Do not expect your baby-sitter or day care to enforce patching in your absence," notes Dr. Gross.

Take care to prevent peeking. Only an occlusion patch prescribed by your eye doctor should be used to treat amblyopia, according to Dr. Gross. These patches come in two sizes and have adhesive all around, so the patch can be firmly stuck to the face to prevent peeking. The junior size is for children up to age five or so. Older children generally use the regular-size patch. It's important to securely fix the patch to the child's face and not to glasses, says Dr. Gross. "If the patch is attached to glasses, the child will be able to peek around the edges with the good eye, and the weak eye will not be challenged enough," he says.

Stick to your guns. Enforce patching to the best of your ability. "Both parents have to be absolutely committed to the pro-

STRAIGHT TALK ABOUT CROSSED EYES

Crossed eyes might look funny on a teddy bear, but for a real-life child with this problem, it's nothing to laugh at. "An inward-turning eye is one of the most common forms of misalignment," says Sherwin Isenberg, M.D., professor and vice chairman of the Department of Ophthalmology at the University of California, Los Angeles, UCLA School of Medicine and the Jules Stein Eye Institute. "If left untreated for too long, the eye never develops full vision potential."

It's important to seek help early. "If your child is born with an eye that crosses all the time, see your doctor right away," says Dr. Isenberg. If an ophthalmologist determines that surgery is necessary, he will probably recommend that the operation be performed relatively soon, according to Dr. Isenberg.

Sometimes, a family photograph can help you detect strabismus (crossed eyes) in a young child, according to Kathleen Mahon, M.D., a pediatric ophthalmologist, clinical professor of pediatrics and surgery at the University of Nevada School of Medicine and director of the Mahon Eye Center, both in Las Vegas. If you see a photograph of your child in which her eyes appear to be different colors, it may indicate that one eye is slightly crossed. Get it checked, suggests Dr. Mahon.

cess of patching. No matter what happens, the child has to comply," says Dr. Gross. "Be very consistent and very strict. Never make any exceptions. If you make one exception, that destroys your credibility with the child," he says.

Manage misbehavior. Dr. Gross offers three suggestions for dealing with kids who misbehave and refuse to wear their patch as prescribed. First, be consistent with your discipline. "Treat misbehavior with patching the same way you would treat any other type of misbehavior," he says. If you use a "time-out" or "go-to-your-room" tactic at other times, use it with patching mischief, too.

Second, deduct any time spent in patchless misbehaving from your child's daily patch-time quota. "That time doesn't count toward patch time, and the child will have to make it up. As soon as he realizes that, the behavior should stop," says Dr. Gross.

Third, if a child takes the patch off for an activity, then that activity should not be allowed. "If a child takes the patch off when he's watching TV, for example, then don't let him watch TV," says Dr. Gross.

Go down for the count. Don't skimp on patch time. "If a child removes the patch even a little bit before the designated time, have him put it back on. If you're not sure how long it's been off, have him start over," says Dr. Gross. "And if patching is not completed one day, then make up for the lost time by adding time the next day."

Talk to the teacher about teasing. A patch can make a kid the butt of many a joke. So if patch time must be during the school day, enlist the aid of your child's teacher, says Dr. Sanet. "The teacher can give a lesson on how we are all different, that there are short people and tall people, fat people and thin. He can make the point that differences, such as wearing glasses or patches, are just differences, and do not make people better or worse than others."

Alert the school nurse. Send the school nurse a "patching report card," suggests pediatric ophthalmologist Kathleen Mahon, M.D., clinical professor of pediatrics and surgery at the University of Nevada School of Medicine and director of the Mahon Eye Center, both in Las Vegas. It should explain what the child's vision problem is and note the hours that the child should be patching. "Ask for the nurse's and the teacher's assistance. It helps to have someone at school who checks on the child," she says.

LICE

Yes, any child—even yours—*can* get a case of lice. And, no, it does not necessarily mean that your child is unclean. Lice, in fact, are almost as easy for kids to get as the common cold. There's a potential for lice whenever children are in a group.

"About 10 million cases of head lice occur each year, and three-quarters of them are in children under the age of 12," says Edward DeSimone, Ph.D., a pharmacist and associate professor of pharmacy and administrative and social sciences in the School of Pharmacy and Allied Health Professions at Creighton University in Omaha.

The first clue that your child may have lice is an itchy scalp. But to see the real evidence, you have to take a close look at your child's head. While you seldom see the lice themselves, their eggs, or nits, are easily visible. These grayish-white oval-shaped eggs attach firmly to the hair shaft. They're tiny, about the size of a sesame seed, and won't wash or blow off, as a flake of skin would.

Effective remedies are as near as the corner drugstore. Here's what the experts suggest you do.

Buy an OTC head-lice product. You can banish the invaders with many over-the-counter products such as RID, A-200, R & C and NIX, says Dr. DeSimone. "All these products are similar," he explains. "They're either a combination of two chemicals—pyrethrin and piperonyl butoxide—working together or they contain a synthetic pyrethrin." The products come in shampoo, liquid or gel form.

The instructions on the package should be followed explicitly because all of these products are pesticides, says Dr. DeSimone. (And experts advise against buying lice sprays because they expose your child to too much pesticide.

Consider a trim. Although it's not necessary to cut a child's hair just because she has lice, shorter hair can be easier to deal with, says Deborah Altschuler, president and cofounder of the National Pediculosis Association in Newton, Massachusetts, and adjunct assistant professor of preventive medicine and bio-metrics at the Uniformed Services University, R. Edward Hébert School of Medicine in Bethesda, Maryland. Remember, however, you cannot take a child with lice to a barber or hairdresser.

Wash hair over the sink. This way you can confine treat-ment to the scalp, says Altschuler. You don't want to use lice prod-ucts in the shower, where the rinsed-off solution can cascade over the body. "These products are pesticides and should be used with caution," she says.

Before you begin, remove your child's shirt and provide a small towel to cover her face. If the product gets in your child's eyes, flush them thoroughly with water right away. Don't be alarmed if some mild skin irritation and itching result from the lice killer, however, and don't mistake this itching for reinfestation.

Be a nit-picker. The lice product will kill the lice, but not all the nits, says Mary Meland, M.D., a pediatrician with Health-Partners in Bloomington, Minnesota. "The more nits you can re-move, the less likelihood there is of a recurrence a couple of weeks later," says Dr. Meland. Also you won't run the risk of mistaking an old nit for a new nit, adds Altschuler.

For nit removal, use a nit removal comb. While there will be a comb packaged with the lice-control product, some work better than others. If the comb is not effective, you can remove the nits with a pair of baby safety scissors (with rounded ends) to cut off the hair that has nits attached.

After the delousing treatment, when your child's hair is dry or only slightly damp, comb it out, then use an old toothbrush and water to remove the nits from the nit comb. If your child used a towel or bathrobe, pop these items into a hot water wash right away, along with any clothes he was wearing before the treatment, then dry them in a hot dryer.

Treat everyone who's infested at the same time. It takes only one little louse to infest a child (they lay up to ten eggs a day), and lice can easily spread from one person to another. So to get rid of these critters you need to examine everyone in the household for signs of lice, says Altschuler, and treat those who are infested.

Make a clean sweep. Once you've detected the lice and treated your children, you need to tend to the household. First, gather up everything washable that has come in contact with your child's head. "This means hats, scarves, hooded coats, hair bands and any clothing your child may have worn in the past few days," says Altschuler. Enlist your child's cooperation in doing this. Don't forget sheets, pillowcases and towels. Wash all items in hot water and dry in a hot dryer.

What you can't wash, you can vacuum or send to the dry cleaners. Vacuum sofas, sofa pillows, mattresses and rugs (especially around the beds), and then put the vacuum cleaner bag in a plastic bag and throw it away. To clean combs and brushes, soak them in hot (not boiling) water for ten minutes.

Take care of Teddy. Yes, the stuffed animals your child hugs and plays with also have to be treated. You can carefully vacuum your child's favorite animals so she'll have them to keep her company, and pop the rest into a large plastic trash bag. Seal the bag tightly with a twist-tie and put the bagged toys away where your child can't get at them.

Generally, lice can't survive off the scalp for more than 24 hours, but it takes the eggs 7 to 10 days to hatch. Therefore, keep the bag sealed for 14 days, says Dr. DeSimone. "After that time, any lice or nits that may have been on the toys will be dead," he says. Any items such as headphones that can't be thoroughly washed or vacuumed should be given the same two-weeks-in-a-bag treatment, according to Dr. DeSimone. Just be sure to keep all bagged items away from small children because of the hazard of choking.

Check daily. Inspect every child in your house for nits every day for at least seven to ten days after treatment, in case you missed a few. "Check for nits throughout the hair, but pay particular attention to behind the ears and the nape of the neck," says Dr. Meland.

If you see new evidence of lice, you'll need to give your child another lice treatment. However, "If you need a second treatment, it should be given seven to ten days after the first treatment," advises Dr. DeSimone.

It's a good idea to make nit-checking part of a regular daily routine even after the lice are long gone, to watch for recurrences. It's easier to vanquish lice if you catch them early.

Teach your child not to share *everything*. All it takes is one hitchhiking louse to make its way from a hat or brush onto another child. "We all want our children to share their belongings," says Dr. DeSimone. "But children should be taught *never* to share combs, brushes, hats, hair ornaments and headphones." Explain to your children why they shouldn't share these items, and make sure each child has his own comb and brush. In fact, your child should have an extra comb and extra brush to take along to school so he won't be tempted to borrow them.

MEASLES

Measles is a viral infection that was once one of the most common childhood illnesses. But thanks to the measles vaccine, it is relatively rare in the United States today. Kids still do get the measles, though, if they aren't immunized. So if your child did not get the vaccine, he may very well come down with this unpleasant virus.

Measles starts out like the common cold, with a cough, runny nose, red and watery eyes and a mild to moderate fever. But you should suspect your child has measles rather than a cold if you detect tiny white spots on the inside of the cheeks. Give the doctor a call.

Sometimes children with measles develop an ear infection, pneumonia or neurological complications. Most of the time, though, kids with measles just feel really sick for seven to ten days. There's not really much you can do about it, except to try to relieve some of the symptoms.

Ease the fever with medication. Give your child a nonaspirin pain reliever such as Children's Tylenol or Tempra to help reduce fever and irritability, says Blair M. Eig, M.D., a pediatrician in private practice in Silver Spring, Maryland. Check the directions on the package for the correct dosage for your child's age and weight. If your child is under age two, consult your physician. "If your child has a high fever that is really debilitating, your pediatrician may prescribe some ibuprofen," adds Dr. Eig. (But ibuprofen should not be given to children unless you have a doctor's recommendation.)

Try a sponge bath. A sponge bath may also help your child feel more comfortable when the fever is high, says Richard Garcia, M.D., a pediatrician and vice chairman of the Department of Pediatrics and Adolescent Medicine at the Cleveland Clinic Foundation in Ohio. Have your child sit in a tub that's partially filled with lukewarm water, and gently sponge the water over his neck and shoulders.

Be generous with beverages. "Give your child plenty of liquids, as much as she can tolerate, preferably juice, Gatorade or Jell-O, which turns to liquid in the stomach," says Betti Hertzberg, M.D., a pediatrician and head of the Continuing Care Clinic at Miami Children's Hospital. "Beverages are important—with high fever and sweating, kids tend to get dehydrated more quickly," Dr. Hertzberg says.

Control the cough when necessary. You can try a mild cough suppressant that contains dextromethorphan to relieve the cough, especially if it's interfering with your child's sleep, suggests Dr. Eig. Over-the-counter products such as Triaminic-DM contain dextromethorphan. Be sure to read package directions—or check with your physician—for the correct dosage for your child.

Make the most of mist. "A cool mist vaporizer will put some humidity in the room air and make it easier for your child to breathe freely," Dr. Garcia says. If you do use a vaporizer, though, you must clean it daily. "Otherwise, bacteria and mold could grow in the still water," he cautions.

Keep the lights low. With measles, the eyes can become very irritated and sensitive to light. "Keep the lights dim in your child's room, or give him sunglasses to wear," advises Dr. Hertzberg.

Flush and wipe the eyes. "Rinsing the eyes with plain saline solution—available at drugstores—may be soothing," says Dr. Eig. Use an eyedropper to put several drops in the corner of each eye.

If your child's eyes get crusty, wipe them with cotton balls that have been wrung out with boiled water, says Dr. Hertzberg. "Be sure to wipe from the inside corner of the eye to the outside, and use a different cotton ball for each eye," she says.

Restrict activity. Be sure that your child stays indoors, preferably in bed, says Dr. Hertzberg. "With the measles, he'll probably feel too sick to do much else," she says.

MOTION SICKNESS

It's one of life's mysteries. Some kids can rocket through the air upside down on amusement park rides, screaming with glee and without a twinge of discomfort, while other kids get pale, clammy, dizzy, nauseated and thoroughly sick just riding in a car.

Some kids, unfortunately, are more susceptible to motion sickness than others. And for parents of kids who are prone to motion sickness, that long vacation trip can turn into a series of roadside stops. Some families don't dare go anywhere without a sickness bag handy.

But what causes the sickness-prone kid to feel this bad?

Actually, it's not only motion that makes her sick but her perception of motion. Here's what happens.

Motion sickness occurs when the brain receives conflicting messages from the inner ears (which control balance and equilibrium) and the eyes, says Mark D. Widome, M.D., professor of pediatrics at Pennsylvania State University Children's Hospital in Hershey. A child reading a book in the back seat of a car, for example, will feel the motion of the car but will not see the motion, since her view is focused on the printed page on her lap.

As unpleasant as motion sickness is, it has no lasting effects. Treatment varies from child to child, and therapies fall into a category that Robert Mendelson, M.D., a pediatrician and clinical professor of pediatrics at Oregon Health Sciences University in Portland, calls WW—whatever works. The WW options may also work if you're traveling in a plane or boat—but car travel is the most common troublemaker. So here are some tactics for the open road.

Make frequent stops. Since many kids don't get sick during the first 30 minutes or so of a car trip, the more stops you make, the less likely your child will become ill. So stop *before* you hear the first cry of "Mommy, I don't feel so good," Dr. Widome advises. "When you stop, have the child get out of the car to get some fresh air and walk around a bit," says Dr. Widome.

Crack the window. Fresh air seems to make a queasy child feel a bit better. So open the window a bit on car trips, even if it's cold outside, advises Dr. Mendelson.

Pass up heavy, greasy meals. A bellyful of greasy French fries or a double cheese pizza is just asking for motion sickness. And once your child is nauseated, points out Dr. Mendelson, the sight or smell of any food may be more than he can tolerate. Carry along some sandwiches, crackers and crunchy vegetables rather than relying on fast food. And avoid any grease-laden meal before the trip begins.

Learn what your child can stomach. Try feeding your child *something* before one trip and *nothing* before another, then see which works better. Some children travel better with an empty stomach, while some do better if they've had dry toast or crackers or something to drink, says Dr. Mendelson.

Be glad for that car seat. For young kids, the car seat is not only a necessary safety measure, it's also a great nausea-prevention device. Children are always less nausea-prone if they can see out the window, according to Dr. Widome.

Furnish a front-row seat. Move the child into the front seat and encourage him to look at cars and buildings far ahead or to look at the horizon. "This way your child will 'see' the same motion that his body and inner ears 'feel,'" says Dr. Mendelson. The other advantage of moving up front is that back seats tend to bounce and sway more, which just may be the final straw for an upset stomach. If kids must sit in the back seat and they're beyond the car seat stage, play some roadside games (like "I see something green") that get them to look out the window.

Nix the printed word. Reading, playing cards or doing homework in the car can prompt motion sickness. Although books with large pictures and only a few words may be okay, your best bet is entertaining your child with music or stories on a tape recorder, says Dr. Mendelson. If you don't have a supply of tapes at home, you can stock up on music and stories at your public library before a long trip.

Beware of fumes. Cigarette, pipe or cigar smoke can make an already queasy child lose his lunch. But Dr. Widome notes that any perfumes or automobile or bus exhausts can also be offensive to your child. If you're following diesel trucks down a busy highway, adjust the ventilation or air conditioning to keep road fumes *out.*

Go for the OTCs. Many over-the-counter antinausea medicines such as Dramamine and Marezine may be effective with your child. These products are primarily antihistamines, and many come in children's formulations as chewable tablets or liquids. These are given *before* the trip.

"Talk to your pediatrician to find out if one of these is appropriate for your child and what dosage to give," says Dr. Mendelson. These work for many children but may make your child drowsy. Never give your child an antinausea medication without a doctor's approval, especially if the child is taking any other medication, because the drugs could interact and cause problems.

MUMPS

Remember having the mumps when you were a kid? Along with feeling weak, headachy and feverish, your parotid glands, located in front of each ear, swelled up on both sides of your face. The swelling was tender and painful, too, and may have lasted from three to seven miserable days.

Most cases of the mumps are unpleasant but not serious. It is possible, however, for mumps to have serious complications, such as infection of the spinal cord and brain, deafness or a painful inflammation of the testicles in teenage and adult males.

The best way to deal with mumps is with prevention. The MMR vaccine protects children from three of the once-common childhood diseases—measles, mumps and rubella. It is now recommended that children receive two doses of MMR, the first at 15 months of age and the second later in childhood. Unfortunately, not every child gets the necessary immunizations, and if yours is among them, it is quite possible that she'll contract the disease.

If your child does come down with mumps, the only thing you can do, besides checking with the doctor, is keep her comfortable. Here's how.

Treat the pain. "Give your child acetaminophen for fever and discomfort," suggests Lorry Rubin, M.D., chief of the Division of Pediatric Infectious Diseases at Schneider Children's Hospital of Long Island Jewish Medical Center in New Hyde Park, New York, and associate professor of pediatrics at the Albert Einstein School of Medicine in New York City. Check the package directions for the correct dosage for your child's age and weight. If your child is under age two, consult a physician.

Make meals moist. "The parotid glands produce saliva, but during the mumps, they can't work as efficiently to moisten the food your child is eating," says Jack H. Hutto, Jr., M.D., chief of pediatric infectious disease at All Children's Hospital in Saint Petersburg, Florida. "If chewing is a chore, offer your child foods with a high liquid content: soup, ice cream, pudding, a slush drink or Cream of Wheat," suggests Dr. Hutto.

Don't be tart. "Avoid giving your child citrus fruits or juices, or any other food that is high in acid," says Dr. Rubin. "Acidic foods stimulate the parotid gland to secrete saliva, a painful process during the mumps."

Go bland on food, too. "Spicy foods provoke contractions of the salivary glands and increase discomfort, so your child will appreciate a bland diet," says Edgar O. Ledbetter, M.D., former chairman of the Department of Pediatrics at Texas Tech University in Lubbock. "Of course, most children realize this as soon as they eat something spicy," since the spiciness almost instantly leads to greater pain.

Shower some extra affection. Spend as much time with your child as you can. "Reading a story, talking, singing or rocking can help make her feel better," says Dr. Hutto.

NIGHT TERRORS AND NIGHTMARES

You're awakened by a blood-curdling scream. You race to your child's room to find her sitting bolt upright in bed, howling, her eyes wide open and filled with terror. You call her name, but she stares right through you, as if you aren't there. She may begin thrashing and striking out. She may even try to get out of bed. Then as suddenly as it began, the "spell" is over and she's sound asleep.

"Most parents who witness this say the child looks like she's possessed," says Barbara Howard, M.D., assistant clinical professor of pediatrics at Duke University Medical Center in Durham, North Carolina. "But there's a perfectly rational explanation. The child is experiencing a night terror."

Though night terrors may sound like something that requires professional help, they are actually normal and fairly common in children. Experts say they occur during the deepest part of the sleep cycle, about an hour or two after the child falls asleep.

"Normally, this is the point where the child cycles into a lighter sleep where dreams occur," says Ronald Dahl, M.D., director of the Children's Sleep Evaluation Center at Western Psychiatric Institute and Clinic in Pittsburgh and associate professor of psychiatry and pediatrics at the University of Pittsburgh Medical Center. "But particularly if the child is very tired, a split may occur. Part of the system says it's time to go into light sleep, but another part says, 'No, I'm still tired.' So part of the brain stays deeply asleep while another part goes into a high-arousal state."

The child who is having a night terror is not awake, yet not quite asleep, notes Dr. Dahl. And the "terror" aspect of this phenomenon really registers only on the parents. The child herself is not conscious, nor does she remember playing out this scene from *The Exorcist* the next day, says Dr. Dahl.

Nightmares, on the other hand, are very frightening for children. "A nightmare is essentially a dream that is sufficiently scary to wake a child up," says Dr. Dahl. "In fact, the child may wake up quickly, become fully awake and have trouble getting back to sleep. He may be a little confused, but he'll probably be coherent. A nightmare is likely to occur late in the night or early in the morning, in the second half of the sleep period."

Both night terrors and nightmares tend to run their course and disappear over time. But there are a few techniques you can use to make things easier for your child.

Stay calm. "Remind yourself that although a night terror looks scary, it's not a seizure. It's not a terrible thing," says Dr. Dahl. "Night terrors are very common and normal, especially in kids between the ages of three and five."

Stand by until it's over. Though it may be difficult to watch your child screaming, there's really nothing you can do to stop a night terror, says Dr. Howard. "But you can make sure the child is safe when it's happening by restraining her if necessary. Children do sometimes hurt themselves thrashing or running around. And it's almost impossible to wake them."

Don't mention it. "Don't talk to your child about the episode the next morning," says Dr. Howard. "And don't let siblings talk to her about it either. Kids don't remember night terrors. But if they find out later what they did, they may get upset about being out of control."

Try a preventive wake-up call. "If your child is experiencing terrors, you could try waking her up about 30 minutes after she goes to bed, and then letting her go back to sleep," says Dr. Howard. "That breaks up the sleep cycle and tends to interrupt the pattern of the night terrors."

Make sure your child is getting enough sleep. "Increase the total amount of sleep your child is getting," suggests Dr. Dahl. "If she's fairly young, it might mean letting her go back to taking daily naps. For an older kid, try letting her sleep longer in the morning or put her to bed a little earlier."

The reason for this, Dr. Dahl explains, is that the more tired a child is, the more difficult it will be for her to switch from deep sleep to light sleep. "The classic time for night terrors to occur is when young children first give up their daily naps," he says. "The first time a kid stays up for 12 hours or more, there's more pressure on her sleep system than she's ever had, and it drives her deeply into sleep, deeper than she's ever been. At the end of that first deep sleep cycle is when she's most likely to have a night terror."

Talk over fears during the day. "Help your child express her worries and fears during the day rather than letting them surface at night," says Dr. Dahl. "Often a child who gets night terrors has a small, specific but irrational fear that's worrying her. As soon as she expresses her fear and understands that it's not worth worrying over, the night terrors go away."

Don't make it a habit. "Be careful to avoid what's called secondary gain, which means the child gets some benefit from having had a night terror," says Dr. Howard. "Even though the night terror was unintentional, if the child wakes up and finds the parent there, concerned about her and giving her a lot of attention, it can seem like a reward. That can reinforce and perpetuate the problem. So it's important not to coddle the child too much—by waking her and giving her something to eat or drink, for instance."

Turn on the light. If a child wakes up with a nightmare and comes running to your room, be prepared to listen and find out why the child is afraid.

"Most kids want their parents around," says Dr. Dahl. "Some don't need much more than your reassurance that everything is all right." But sometimes, you may have to go back to the child's room, turn on the light and show him there's nothing there. "The child really needs to spend more time with you until he winds down," says Dr. Dahl.

HOW TO STOP A SLEEPWALKER

Watching your child perambulate around the house while in a deep sleep can be an unsettling experience, but it's anything but rare.

Sleepwalking, like night terrors, usually occurs during a child's transition from very deep to light, dreaming sleep, says Ronald Dahl, M.D., director of the Children's Sleep Evaluation Center at Western Psychiatric Institute and Clinic in Pittsburgh and associate professor of psychiatry and pediatrics at the University of Pittsburgh Medical Center.

"This is a very difficult transition for young children to make, and they often do strange things, like sleepwalking or talking in their sleep," says Dr. Dahl. If you have a sleepwalker, safety is the primary concern. Here's what the experts recommend you do.

- Wake up the child. "You can often wake up a child from sleepwalking and guide him back to bed," says Barbara Howard, M.D., clinical assistant professor of pediatrics at Duke University Medical Center in Durham, North Carolina.
- Increase sleep time. "Being overtired is a major factor in sleepwalking," notes Dr. Dahl. "Ninety-nine percent of children experiencing these partial arousals do better after increasing the total amount of sleep."
- Install a gate. "Install a portable, folding gate or a screen door to block the doorway so he can't get out," suggests Dr. Howard. "These are better than locking the door and you can hear him if he gets up." You should also place a gate across any stairways.
- Change bed arrangements. "If your child is sleeping in a bunk bed, make sure you take him off the top bunk," advises Dr. Dahl.

Break the rules now and then. Your child may want to spend the rest of the night in your bed, even if it's not usually allowed. "It's okay to occasionally break the rules if the child is badly frightened," says Dr. Dahl, "though you may have to nip that behavior in the bud before it becomes a bad habit. Most kids will go back to their bed without protest the next night if you remind them of the rule."

Give the child a nightmare protector. A flashlight or a "protective" stuffed animal can be very soothing to a child plagued by nightmares, says Sheila Ribordy, Ph.D., a clinical psychologist specializing in treating children and families and professor of psychology and director of clinical training in the Department of Psychology at DePaul University in Chicago.

"For a child, it's important to feel he has some control over his nightmares," she says. "Children need to have a sense that they are powerful people so things aren't so scary for them."

Have a bedside chat. "If a child is having a lot of nightmares, you may need to help him relieve some of the stress that comes up during the day," says Dr. Howard. "Children these days are under enormous stress. Often they're watching violent movies or TV programs. Sometimes they're subjected to a bully at school or at day care. Or they're being asked to toilet train or deal with a new sibling or give up their room." Since these stresses can lead to nightmares, it helps if you can talk to your child about what's happened during the day, according to Dr. Howard.

Follow a calming bedtime routine. "Your child's experience at bedtime should be a calming one," says Dr. Howard. She suggests including a story, a song or cuddly animals in the routine.

Children who are having nightmares may develop a fear of falling asleep, and a bedtime routine that includes books or music can help. "Playing music or story tapes gives them something to focus on other than the fear of nightmares that might be coming," says Dr. Ribordy. "Often these activities are distracting enough to help them fall asleep easily."

PINWORMS

There's a voice coming from the darkness next to your bed and it doesn't belong to the morning radio newscaster. "I can't sleep," it says in that whining pitch you know oh-so-well. So you turn on the light and find your child standing there, scratching his pajama bottoms. This is the third morning in a row that he's been a walking alarm clock, rousing you before 6:30 A.M. with complaints of itching.

If this scenario sounds familiar, your child may have pinworms.

Pinworms are a type of intestinal nematode (a round worm) that live only in people. In the United States, they are the most common worm infection. "Pinworms are quite prevalent," says Robert Pond, M.D., physician with the Epidemic Intelligence Service at the Centers for Disease Control and Prevention in Atlanta. "Studies show that between 10 and 30 percent of children get them."

Because pinworms lay microscopic, infectious eggs that can spread from person to person, the problem is easy to pass along, says J. Owen Hendley, M.D., professor of pediatrics and head of pediatric infectious diseases at the University of Virginia School of Medicine in Charlottesville. Pinworms take up residence in the large intestine of an infected child. At night or in the early morning, the female worms travel down to the anal opening and deposit their eggs on the surrounding skin. When the child scratches the itchy area, pinworm eggs get on his hands and under his fingernails.

Then, if he doesn't wash his hands, the pinworm eggs get on whatever he touches, including toys and other household objects. Other children come along, touch what the infected child touched, and get the eggs on their hands, too. If they stick their hands in their mouth without washing them first, says Dr. Hendley, they can swallow the eggs, get infected, and the next thing you know, those kids have itchy bottoms, too.

Once your doctor has confirmed that your child has pinworms, he'll probably prescribe medication. And, meanwhile, here's what to do yourself.

Reassure your child. The thought of having worms could upset anybody, especially a youngster. So it's important to explain to your child that this does not mean that he is bad or dirty, and that he does not have to be embarrassed. Lots of children get worms.

"These worms do not have much of a mouth. They have no teeth and they can't bite," says J. Martin Kaplan, M.D., professor of clinical pediatrics at Hahnemann University in Philadelphia. He recommends saying to your child, "There is nothing to be afraid of. You can't be hurt. The only thing you will be bothered by is some itching, and the medicine the doctor has given you should take that away."

Put water to work against itching. If your child has a lot of itching, taking a bath or wiping the anal area with a moist cloth can bring some temporary relief, says Janice Woolley, M.D., a pediatrician in private practice in Mercer Island, Washington. But be sure to keep that cloth away from other members of the family—and wash your own hands thoroughly if you touch it.

Buy cartoon-y soap. To stop pinworm from spreading and to prevent reinfection, you should take steps to emphasize cleanliness. Good hand-washing habits are particularly important, says Dr. Kaplan. If your child is potty training, encourage hand washing by overseeing her. Buy a soap that she will relate to and want to play with, such as soap in the shape of a cartoon character, he says.

Keep nails cut short. Regularly trimming back your child's fingernails can also help, adds Dr. Woolley. Long fingernails provide convenient hiding places for eggs in transit. If you cut them short, it's easier for the child to wash up thoroughly—and wash away those eggs.

Practice moderation. Emphasize good hygiene, but don't go overboard. "You can wash your child's anal area, but don't scrub too hard in an effort to achieve ultra-cleanliness," says

THE DETECTIVE WORK IS UP TO YOU

Experts say that the best way to pin the rap on pinworms is for parents to collect the hard evidence themselves.

While your child is sleeping, spread the cheeks of his buttocks and look at the anal opening with a flashlight. Sometimes you can see the female worms, which are a whitish color and about ¼ to ⅓ inch long. "They look like a small piece of cotton," says J. Martin Kaplan, M.D., professor of pediatrics at Hahnemann University in Philadelphia.

If you can catch one with a pair of tweezers, stick it in a bottle or small plastic bag and take it to your doctor, says Dr. Kaplan. But even if you're not quick enough to nab a worm, be sure to tell the doctor that you've seen one, he says.

You may be able to collect a sample of pinworm eggs from a sleeping child by pressing a piece of cellophane tape against the skin around the anal opening. You can't see the eggs, but if they're there, the tape will pick them up. Seal the potential evidence onto the tape by placing it on a glass slide (which you can get from your doctor or buy at the drugstore) sticky side down. Take this to your doctor, who will look for the presence of eggs under a microscope.

Usually, the detective work doesn't even wake kids up, says Dr. Kaplan. You can also check when your child comes to you complaining of itching, or first thing in the morning before your child has had her bath.

Donald Gromisch, M.D., professor and chairman of the Department of Pediatrics at Nassau County Medical Center in East Meadow, New York, and professor of pediatrics at the State University of New York at Stony Brook. Scrubbing can be counterproductive if it irritates the child's behind, he says.

PRICKLY HEAT

You are taking your two-week-old for her first ride in the stroller on a mild spring day. Although the thermometer is registering 61° F, the breeze feels chilly. So you carefully dress your baby in a long-sleeved T-shirt, overalls and a lovely pink angora hat and jacket knitted by Great Aunt Edith. You also tuck her under a blanket.

Your walk goes well, and you both enjoy the fresh air. But when you get home, it's a while before you divest your daughter of all those extra clothes. When you do, you notice a fine, pink rash on her neck and upper back. What you're looking at is called prickly heat, the end result of too much heat with no place to go.

"When a baby gets hot, sweat must evaporate off the skin in order to cool her body down," says Scott A. Norton, M.D., a staff dermatologist at Tripler Army Medical Center in Honolulu. "If you interfere with this process by covering the skin with lots of clothing, plastic pants or even heavy moisturizers, the sweat that needs to get out becomes trapped beneath the surface of the skin, resulting in an itchy rash."

Newborns are particularly vulnerable to prickly heat because their sweat ducts are not mature, which makes it easier for the beads of moisture to be trapped, says Dr. Norton.

Although prickly heat is common in babies, who are unable to complain about being overdressed, older kids can get the rash, too. Fortunately, it's easy to treat and even easier to prevent. Here's how.

Don't overdress your child. "While prickly heat can sometimes occur as the result of fever, the most common cause is overdressing or swaddling a baby tightly in warm blankets," says Dr. Norton. Dress your baby sensibly—preferably in layers that can be peeled away as conditions change—and you'll likely avoid the problem altogether, he says.

Avoid heavy moisturizers. Tender newborn skin tends to be dry and in need of moisturizing. But heavy, oil-based creams can be a problem, notes Dr. Norton. "Moisturize with a light, water-based lotion instead," he advises. Moisturel, Lubriderm and Alpha-Keri body oil are some of the moisturizers you can use.

Keep cotton in contact with skin. Plastic is a great material for keeping wetness out, but it also traps moisture in the skin. "Let your child's skin breathe by using cotton rather than plastic diaper wraps, and by covering plastic mattress and playpen covers with cotton ones," says Sam Solis, M.D., chairman of the Department of Pediatrics at Children's Hospital, and an assistant professor of pediatrics at Tulane University School of Medicine, both in New Orleans, and a pediatrician in Metarie, Louisiana.

Bring the temperature down. The first step in treating prickly heat once it develops is to get your child to stop sweating. "Remove some clothing, take her into an air-conditioned room or sit her in a tub of tepid water," suggests Dr. Solis. (The water should be just a little warmer than skin temperature.)

Soak away the itch. To counter the itching that accompanies prickly heat, add some baking soda or a colloidal oatmeal product such as Aveeno Bath Treatment to a tub of tepid water, suggests Betti Hertzberg, M.D., a pediatrician and head of the Continuing Care Clinic at Miami Children's Hospital.

"Have your child splash around in the tub for a while," says Dr. Hertzberg. "A good soak will soothe the skin and take away the itching."

Try a cool compress. While a thin coating of mild, water-based moisturizing lotion may help stop the itching, cool compresses sometimes work better. Make a compress by dipping a washcloth in a mixture of 1 teaspoon of baking soda per cup of cool water, suggests Dr. Hertzberg. Apply to the rash for five to ten minutes or as long as your child can tolerate it. This should be done four or five times a day, Dr. Hertzberg says.

Bed down with an antihistamine. If your child is extremely itchy, give her an itch-relieving antihistamine such as Benadryl Elixir before she goes to sleep, suggests Dr. Hertzberg. (Be sure to read package directions to make certain the product is recommended for your child's age. For the correct dosage, follow package directions or consult your physician. Some doctors don't advise Benadryl cream or spray because it could cause a reaction.) "Kids are much more sensitive to itchiness at night, and more likely to scratch the rash, which can lead to infection," she says.

Apply a hydrocortisone cream. "For kids aged three or older, soothe the itch with a light coating of 1 percent hydrocortisone cream," says Dr. Norton. "You can apply this over-the-counter remedy twice a day for two days to soothe itching and relieve inflammation and redness," he says.

Screen the sun without grease. Older kids tend to get prickly heat when they use a heavy, oily sunscreen that clogs sweat pores, notes Dr. Norton. The answer to the problem is *not* to stop using sunscreen, however. "Because of the problems associated with sun exposure, children should always use sunscreen, but it's best to avoid the oily, cocoa butter-laden preparations," says Dr. Norton. In his practice in Hawaii, he advises his patients to use less greasy lotions that are hypoallergenic, block UVA and UVB sunlight and are marketed for young children.

SCHOOL REFUSAL

His first month in middle school, Stephen started missing the school bus routinely.

When Jane entered the first grade, she began having painful stomachaches every school morning.

Three-year-old Tyler screamed with anguish whenever his mother left him at preschool.

All these children shared a problem that occurs in many children: They didn't want to go to school. The possible causes range from simple separation anxiety at leaving their parents to serious problems with school, classmates or teacher.

After you've ruled out actual physical ailments, here's how you can deal with the child who doesn't want to go to school.

FOR ALL CHILDREN

Explain the facts. Whatever age your child, you need to explain why the child must go to school, says David Waller, M.D., pediatrician, child psychiatrist and chief of child and adolescent psychiatry at the University of Texas Southwestern Medical Center and Children's Medical Center in Dallas.

For the preschool child, keep it in simple terms: "This is a place where people will take care of you and you can play while we are at work" or "Mommy and Daddy want you to meet new friends, and this is a good place to do it." But make it clear that you're not angry at your child or punishing her.

For older children, explain that it's a law that they attend school. Dr. Waller recommends that you tell them the consequences of missing school or constantly being tardy. If the child knows he may receive poor grades, get detention or possibly have to repeat a year, he's more likely to climb on that morning bus.

Visit the school. For the child just starting preschool or kindergarten or transferring to a new school, arrange a visit before the first day.

"Spend some time in the classroom with your child," says Karen Smith, Ph.D., a pediatric psychologist and associate professor of pediatrics in the School of Medicine at the University of Texas Medical Branch in Galveston. "Talk to the teacher, too, so that your child can see that Mom and Dad like this new person, that she's not someone to be afraid of. You might need to do this more than once for very anxious children," she says.

Supply a map. Children can worry a great deal about finding their way around a strange place. Draw a map of the school in bright colors for your child and point out places such as the art room, bathroom and lunchroom. Hang the map on the wall of your child's room.

"It's important for your child to become familiar with the physical layout of any new school," says Leah Klungness, Ph.D., a psychologist in Locust Valley, New York. "Not being able to find the bathroom can upset a child who is already shaky about new beginnings."

Tantalize with descriptions. Find out what types of activities your child's preschool or school will have, and describe them to your child. "Talk to your child about the kinds of things he'll be doing there and the friends he'll make," suggests Dr. Smith. "Try to find something of interest that will happen in that setting that might not happen at home." For example, if your child will learn to fingerpaint at preschool or have recess every day at kindergarten, explain that to him.

JUST FOR PRESCHOOLERS

Depart cheerfully. This means no prolonged leave-takings with smothering hugs and kisses and syrupy reassurances. "Don't tell your child, for example, that he shouldn't be afraid or that nothing bad will happen to him," says Dr. Waller. "If a child reads anxiety in a parent, he's bound to think that there must be something to be anxious about."

Give a quick kiss and a hug, tell your child when you will return and leave with a smile on your face—whether or not your child is screaming and beseeching you to come back.

Leave openly. Although it may seem easiest to sneak off while your child is playing quietly, don't do it. "Whether your child is howling or playing quietly, never just disappear," says Cathleen A. Rea, Ph.D., a clinical child psychologist at Riverside Regional Medical Center and the Behavioral Medicine Institute in Newport News, Virginia, and assistant professor in the Department of Psychiatry and Behavioral Science at Eastern Virginia Medical School in Norfolk. "That's traumatic to a child; Mommy or Daddy disappearing is his worst fear. You need to let him know when you're leaving."

Plant a lipstick kiss. Preschool children may find a lipstick imprint from Mom comforting. "Cover your lips with lipstick and then kiss your child on her hand or wrist where she can see the lipstick imprint," suggests Dr. Klungness. "Lipstick doesn't wash off so easily, so it's a constant reminder of your presence."

Supply pictures of Mom and Dad. A small photo of his parents tacked into his cubby or locker may be immensely comforting. "A picture showing you in your office or workplace is particularly helpful," says Dr. Klungness. "Looking at that picture, the child sees you in a particular physical environment, and he won't feel as if you've disappeared."

Arrange for a greeting. It's important that you don't just drop your child off in a crowd of children, says Dr. Rea. "When you walk into the day care center, you want to have a teacher or aide come over immediately to greet you and your child. She should get down to eye level and help with the transition from parent to day care setting," she says. At a busy day care center, you may have to make a request in advance but most caregivers will be happy to cooperate with this greeting arrangement.

Provide a time framework. Very young children often don't have a good sense of time, so telling your child a specific activity you will do together that evening will help her realize that day care isn't forever. "You could tell her that you'll stop for a snack on the way home, or that you'll read her favorite book while dinner is cooking," suggests Dr. Rea.

Take Teddy along. It can make day care far less frightening to take along a favorite toy. "Bringing any special transitional object from home is often comforting to an anxious child," says Dr. Rea.

Ask about your child's behavior. After a few weeks you may feel that things aren't getting any better. Your child still screams and cries when you leave. But once you're out of sight—unknown to you—he may be playing happily the rest of the day.

"Check with your child's teacher to find out if there's a decrease in the intensity and the duration of the emotional distress your child experiences," suggests Dr. Smith. If your child adjusts rapidly after you leave, stop worrying.

FOR OLDER CHILDREN

Talk it out. Talk gently with your child to find out what is bothering him about school, suggests Dr. Klungness. If you can't discover the problem, arrange a conference with the teacher. There could be a bully who has been picking on your child. Other children could be taunting him because of the style of his clothing. He may be anxious because he feels he's not doing well in school. Or something could have happened that embarrassed him. Dr. Rea counseled one child who refused to go to school after he dropped his lunch tray in the cafeteria. "It can be as innocuous as that," she says.

Think about things at home. A sudden change in your child's school-going behavior can sometimes be traced to events at home. "Consider if there is something going on at home that might have precipitated your child's refusal to go to school," advises Dr. Waller. "Sometimes a child who has experienced a death or illness in the family—or notices her parents' marital problems—feels that she is 'needed' at home and will do what she has to to remain there."

If there is a problem, don't lie to your child about it, but don't go into great detail either, says Dr. Waller. Explain that it is Mommy and Daddy's job to deal with the problem. Your child should understand that it's *her* job to go to school and try to do well. Reassure her that you will be honest with her so she doesn't feel she needs to stay home to know what's going on.

Take charge of real problems. While your child needs to know that every school day won't be perfect and that she has to learn to deal with problems, she also needs to know you will help when needed, says Dr. Klungness.

For instance, if your small child is being tormented or hit by other kids on the bus, talk to the bus driver or principal. If your child is having trouble with schoolwork, set aside time when the two of you can work together on problem areas. And if you become convinced that the teacher has taken a dislike to your child or doesn't want to help solve your child's problems, you should arrange a meeting with the principal to consider transferring your child to another class.

Accentuate the positive. For the child with minor problems, acknowledge what your child dislikes about school, but try to identify some things that she *does* like. Remind her of the music lessons she loves or a friend she sees only at school, says Dr. Smith.

Seek guidance. Talk to the school's guidance counselor or nurse and ask if your child can visit the nurse during the day if she suddenly becomes anxious, suggests Dr. Waller. You don't want to encourage frequent visits, but if the anxious child knows she has someone to turn to, it gives her reassurance. "It's better than coming home early, which would only reinforce the school refusal behavior," says Dr. Waller.

Give praise to your child. Sometimes the best reward is a big hug and a word of praise from Mom and Dad. Be sure to acknowledge your child's efforts. "Your child should be complimented every time she stays through the school day or goes to school without protest," says Dr. Smith.

SEPARATION ANXIETY

For all of us, life is filled with goodbyes—sometimes tearful—but none are so poignant as those experienced by our children. At various developmental stages, preschoolers may exhibit what's known as separation anxiety, usually expressed by crying—even screaming—as we leave them at day care, at school or with a babysitter. Separation anxiety is not only normal, it's also a positive sign that your child is attached to you. But there are ways to take some of the pain and tears out of parting.

Let your child know you're always coming back. "If a mom tells me her child screams every time she leaves, I tell her, 'You don't get away often enough,'" says pediatrician Robert Mendelson, M.D., clinical professor of pediatrics at the Oregon Health Sciences University in Portland. "A child who screams every time his mother leaves may not be sure she's coming back." After several short absences, though, even the most anxious child should get the message that mommy can leave and come back, too.

Prepare the child. Let your child know you will be leaving, even if it causes a little anticipatory anxiety. It's better than a surprise, says Jay Belsky, Ph.D., professor of human development at Pennsylvania State University in University Park. However, he cautions, don't belabor it. "Say simply and casually, 'Mommy and Daddy are going out and the babysitter is coming to stay with you.' If you keep talking about it," says Dr. Belsky, "it will sound like you're anxious, too, and you'll communicate that to your child."

No long goodbyes. "At the point of departure, make it clean and crisp," says Dr. Belsky. "Standing in the doorway cajoling and explaining is the worst thing you can do because it creates more anxiety. Remind yourself that the distress you see at the point of separation is most likely not going to continue after you are gone."

Since it's short, make it sweet. Leaving the child with an "I love you" and a kiss may be helpful. Dr. Belsky suggests that you tuck a "kiss" into the child's pocket as a goodbye ritual.

Acknowledge the child's feelings. Instead of saying, "Now don't cry" or "Don't feel that way"—which betrays your own anxiety over having caused your child distress—acknowledge how the child is feeling and reassure him. "Say 'I know this is difficult for you, but you're a big boy and I know you can do it,'" suggests Dr. Belsky. "Make sure you tell the child that it's okay to feel the way he does."

Leave something of yourself. Whether you give the child something personal, like a piece of jewelry or article of clothing, or start a project that you promise to finish when you return, you're sending the message "I am coming back," says Dr. Belsky. "Anything that sends that message, that preserves continuity and preserves the relationship is a good thing."

Plan some activities. "For the older child—five or so—it's often helpful to structure the time you're going to be away with games and activities because distraction can help children not obsess on the experience," says Sheila Ribordy, Ph.D., a clinical psychologist specializing in children and families, and a professor of psychology and director of clinical training in the Department of Psychology at DePaul University in Chicago.

Leave them with someone they know. Children feel much more secure with a familiar face than with a strange one. If you're using a new babysitter, ask her to come over at least 45 minutes before you leave. And be sure to sit and talk with the babysitter and your child before you walk out the door, suggests Dr. Belsky. "Parents should have a nice friendly conversation, maybe do some laughing with this person. Children usually feel that any friend of Mommy's is a friend of theirs."

SHYNESS

Just as some kids seem born to be wild, others are born to be shy. "Shyness is often a symptom of a cautious temperament, which is hereditary, like blue eyes and curly hair," says Jerome Kagan, Ph.D., a leading shyness researcher and professor of psychology at Harvard University in Cambridge, Massachusetts.

"Unless shyness is interfering with your child's life, don't think of it as a problem," says Dr. Kagan. "Many children outgrow their shyness as they have more social experiences. You don't want your child to believe you are disappointed in him."

But what if shyness has grown to the point where your child is having trouble making friends, is turning down invitations to classmates' parties and never volunteering in class? Then his shyness is a problem that can result in both academic problems and an unhappy social life.

"Shy kids have a hard time asking for help," says Lynne Henderson, Ph.D., director of the Palo Alto Shyness Clinic in Menlo Park, California. "A study of college students found that the shy ones were less likely than their nonshy peers to seek information or use the career placement service. They had a disadvantage which was handicapping their careers."

The experts agree: If your child's shyness is a real problem, the best time to start intervening is as early as possible. Here are some helpful techniques they recommend.

Don't put a label on it. "If you label a child as shy, you only see his shy behavior and tune out what is not shy," says Dr. Henderson. That affects the child's behavior and also affects your perception of him, she notes. Instead, point out the child's strengths. "Focus on the times when a child is being more social, rather than when he's being shy," says Dr. Henderson. Also, use some descriptive words that accentuate the strong points of his behavior, she suggests. For example, a shy person might be better described as cautious, careful or a deep thinker.

Ask for his feelings. Rather than scolding a child for being shy, reflect back to him in a neutral way what he may be feeling, suggests Dr. Henderson. "If he's hiding behind your leg instead of playing with his friends, say, 'It seems like you're not sure you want to play right now.' Something like this might be an accurate reflection of the child's experience but not a negative label," says Dr. Henderson.

Create safe social encounters. Allow the child to invite a schoolmate over after school. Or let him pay a visit to the home of a child he seems to like. "The more comfortable social experiences shy children have, the less anxious they become," says Dr. Kagan.

Be sociable yourself. "When your child is little, work on having people in the home," says Dr. Henderson. Invite friends for a weekend barbecue or a games night. Have another parent and her child over for lunch. "This is often difficult in homes where both parents work, but a shy child needs to get used to an environment with other people in it, so it doesn't seem so frightening."

Stay on standby with your child. For a shy child, large gatherings can be terrifying. "Don't just walk into a room full of people and leave the child standing there," says Dr. Henderson. "Hold onto the child's hand until she gets established. Wait for her to let go." Dr. Henderson recommends that you walk over to another child or a group of children and start talking to them until the child starts talking, too. "A shy child needs to feel secure and to know you're there if she needs you," he notes.

Encourage your child to talk at home. Establish a daily "good news" time. At dinner or bedtime, allow your child to share some good news of the day, suggests Dr. Henderson. "Listen in a nonjudgmental way to what he describes as the high point of his day and then acknowledge his feelings. You might ask what he enjoyed about the experience, but don't load him up with praise.

"This is not a chance to give him an 'A' but a chance to share himself," says Dr. Henderson. "Being listened to and acknowledged with respect helps build self-confidence."

Follow the child's lead. Don't force your child into situations, says Dr. Kagan. Instead, listen carefully to what he says so you can help steer him toward activities and people he's shown an interest in. "You're trying for gentle desensitization, and that only works if the child is doing something he really wants to do."

Add the spice of variety. You never know what activity can spark the interest of a shy child. So be sure to explore the variety of activities available in your community, from swimming lessons to children's theater, suggests Dr. Henderson. This will help you and your child learn where his interests lie. "It's like food. You provide all the basic food groups and the child then can pick and choose."

Enlist the help of a teacher. A receptive, empathetic teacher can help lure your shy child out of the corner into the thick of things or pair him with a friendly classmate who is more outgoing, notes Dr. Henderson. Be sure to let the teacher know you're trying to find activities that will help your child feel good about himself. And show your appreciation for the teacher's help. "If you're really appreciative to a teacher who looks out for your child, she'll do more of it," says Dr. Henderson.

Have a dress rehearsal. Novel situations are a nightmare for shy people, because they generally tend to overestimate danger, says Byron Egeland, Ph.D, professor of child development in the Institute of Child Development at the University of Minnesota in Minneapolis. If your child is going to a party, starting in a new classroom or moving to a new neighborhood, talk about what is going to happen and go over some of the things he may see, hear or do, recommends Dr. Egeland. If possible, visit the new neighborhood or school with your child, talk to his new teachers and also have him meet the other children.

"The more you can familiarize your child with a new situation, the less there is to fear," says Dr. Egeland.

Stay cool, calm and casual. Even if you feel anxiety about a new situation, don't reveal that to your shy child when preparing him for new situations, suggests Dr. Kagan. "Many parents who were shy themselves are really worried their child will relive their unhappiness. They can get so tense that their anxiety is communicated to the child," he notes.

Share your experiences. Since 93 percent of the population acknowledges feeling shy at least once in a while, you no doubt have a story or two to tell about your insecurities. And those stories help a shy child to feel more confident in similar situations.

"Everybody feels shy sometimes. It's the human state," says Dr. Henderson. Share the ways you overcame your insecurities, she says. "Children need to see that this is just part of the everyday human struggle and that you can cope."

Don't demand perfection. "One of the problems we frequently have to work on in the shyness clinic is the belief that being good socially somehow means being perfect all the time," says Dr. Henderson. Shy children need to find out that they can make friends without being perfect. "People think they need to act like movie stars," he notes. "But kids need to know that being friendly doesn't mean being perfect."

SIBLING RIVALRY

So, your kids don't exactly get along like the Waltons. Okay, so they get along more like the World Wrestling Federation. This is normal, right?

Wrong. Although parents can't necessarily recreate the warm, fuzzy feelings the siblings on Walton's Mountain had for each other, there are certainly many ways to avoid full-scale warfare among brothers and sisters. "You can easily make their interaction a better experience by what you do," says child and family psychologist Barry Ginsberg, Ph.D., executive director of the Center of Relationship Enhancement in Doylestown, Pennsylvania.

"There are no easy answers, but it's important to remember that some conflict can be constructive—provided it doesn't get out of hand," says Dr. Ginsberg. "Stresses and fights occur because that's how we negotiate a new, more stable level of relationship. But kids tend to be clumsy at this, and so they need their parents' help."

Here are a few ways to maintain the peace in your household.

Set clear limits. You may not be able to stop your children from arguing, but you can keep disagreements from escalating into brawls, says James Bozigar, a licensed social worker and coordinator of community relations for the Family Intervention Center at Children's Hospital of Pittsburgh. "Make it clear that hitting and the behaviors that often provoke it—name calling, taunting, attacking personal weaknesses—are off limits," he says. "You can say, 'You don't have to love your baby sister, you don't even have to like her, but you must stop hitting her.'"

Call a family powwow. If you're trying to establish new guidelines for behavior, it's better if the siblings themselves play a role in figuring out what those guidelines would be, says Adele Faber, coauthor of *Siblings Without Rivalry*. Faber, who conducts nationwide workshops on sibling relationships, recommends calling a family meeting to do just that.

"Open the floor to discussion," she says. "When it's a rule the child has helped fashion, he'll want to try to make it work. But if it's a rule imposed from on high, he'll be more likely to test or challenge it."

Reinforce the family's new guidelines. If the rule is "no hitting," the disciplinary action for infractions should be a time-out, says Mark Roberts, Ph.D., a professor of psychology at Idaho State University in Pocatello. Dr. Roberts and his colleagues have studied which techniques are most effective in stopping sibling aggression. "Calling time-out wins hands down," he says. "When the kids begin to fight, parents should say, 'No hitting in this house. *You* sit on this chair, and *you* sit on that chair.' The chairs should be up against walls and around the corner from each other so the kids can't see each other. Wait two to five minutes, then talk with the kids about their argument. They will probably have cooled off, so this is a good time to discuss alternatives to fighting."

Substitute words for fists. Brothers and sisters who fight often don't know how to share, take turns, consider others' feelings or negotiate—all skills they're going to need to form relationships outside the home, says Faber. "So one of the rules that is especially helpful is, 'Say it with words, not with fists,'" she says. By using language to express their anger, siblings take the first step on the road to mutually respectful relationships.

Says Faber: "The sweetest thing I heard was from a mother who had tried this method. She called me and said, 'I passed by the kids' room today and saw my older child with his fists raised about to clobber his younger sister. She looked up at him and said, "Michael, use your words." He stopped, with his fists in midair, and said, "Get out of my room!" She said, "I'm going." I was so pleased.' I told that mother, 'Now, *that's* civilized behavior.'"

Don't ask who started it. The usual response to the question "Who started it?" is a two-parter: "He did." "No, she did." But you don't want to play judge or jury, says Faber. "You won't get to the bottom of it. The bottom is bound to be murky. Often you'll hear, 'I had to hit him because I could tell he was about to hit me.'" It's better to say, "Boy, you two sound angry at each other!" That statement diminishes rage and provides an opening for a discussion of the children's real grievances. "So, Adam, you're upset because you want to watch TV. And, Jim, you're upset because you need quiet to study. What can be done in a case like this?"

Reflect feelings back to the child. Very few kids are really happy about sharing their parents' love and attention with someone else, even if that someone else is related to them. Negative feelings toward siblings are normal, says Faber. "It's important to allow those negative emotions to surface. Feelings that are banished don't vanish. They either go underground and get expressed in dreams, nightmares, headaches and stomachaches, or they're acted out in punches or pinches," she says.

Faber suggests listening to your child's feelings and then reflecting them back in a way that acknowledges the child's mixed emotions about a sibling—who is, after all, both an interloper and a playmate. "A father in one of my workshops listened to his son's long list of objections to his new baby sister. Then he reflected back to the boy, 'Sounds to me as if part of you wants her out of here forever. And part of you is sometimes glad she's here.' Periodically over the next few weeks, the little boy said, 'Daddy, tell me again about my two feelings.' I think that child is well on his way to emotional health," says Faber.

Create a special time for one-to-one parenting. "When a new sibling arrives, reserve special times when you can fully commit yourself to being with the older child," says Dr. Ginsberg. "Don't allow any external events to change this. The older child needs to be confident that he will have his special time alone with the parent."

Ask the older child to give you a hand. An older sibling will feel more involved in things if you give her a simple job to do, like bringing you diapers. "This will increase the child's sense of importance and responsibility," says Dr. Ginsberg. "You can say, 'Now that we're busier with the new baby and you're older, you can have this job that will help out around the house.'" Just be sure the task is meaningful—not some busy work invented simply to make the child feel better. "That's phony, and kids can see right through it," Dr. Ginsberg says.

Figure out a way to say "you're special." "Children need to be seen and enjoyed as separate individuals," says Faber. "If you were to say to your husband, 'Who do you love more, your mother or me?' and he replied, 'Honey, I love you both equally,' he would be in big trouble. But if he said, 'Honey, there's no comparison. My mother is my mother and you're my beloved wife,' he'd be on safe ground."

The same policy works for kids. For example, when little Amy asks, "Who do you love best?" you can answer, "Each of my children is special. You are my only Amy. No one has your thoughts, your feelings, your smile, your way of doing things. Boy, am I lucky you are my child."

Respect sibling differences. While it may seem "fair" to give each child the same number of pancakes in the morning, this "fair" treatment doesn't recognize that each child's appetite may be different, says Faber. "If you hear, 'Hey, you gave him three pancakes and you only gave me two,' respond with, 'Oh, are you still hungry? Do you want a whole pancake or just a half? A whole? Well, one whole pancake coming up.' What you've done is shift the message from 'You are getting as much as your big brother' to 'I am meeting your individual needs.'"

STUTTERING

British statesman Sir Winston Churchill was a stutterer, as were scientist Sir Isaac Newton and writer W. Somerset Maugham. So are singer Carly Simon and actors Bruce Willis and James Earl Jones. That your child is in such distinguished company may be small consolation, though. Stuttering is a problem that can affect your child's social life, his school performance and his self-esteem.

There are many theories on why people stutter, but none is conclusive. One thing that is clear is that stuttering—or disfluency, as the experts call it—is a problem of childhood. "Ninety percent of the people who are going to stutter start to do so by the time they're seven," says Edward Conture, Ph.D., a professor of speech-language pathology and chairperson of the Department of Communication Sciences and Disorders at Syracuse University in New York, and one of the nation's leading experts on childhood stuttering.

There is good news: Most children who begin to stutter gradually stop. Therapy with a trained speech and language pathologist tends to be quite successful, says Barry Guitar, Ph.D, professor of communication sciences and disorders at the Eleanor M. Luse Center for Communication Disorders at the University of Vermont College of Arts and Sciences in Burlington.

However, intervention needs to be undertaken early, says Dr. Guitar, himself a stutterer. "With the majority of kids under five, treatment helps so much they will either overcome their problem or have only a minor disfluency. If the stuttering is severe, treatment is usually successful in helping the child learn to deal with it so it doesn't interfere with communication."

Though stuttering generally requires professional help, there are many supplemental things parents can do at home to help their child overcome this relatively common problem. Here are some simple techniques suggested by the experts.

Talk like Mr. Rogers. That means slow down and speak clearly. Although many parents find this television personality's delivery annoying, his rate of speech does closely match kids' speech-processing abilities, according to Dr. Guitar. "On the other hand, if a child is listening to an adult speaking at a very rapid rate, the child will also try to speak rapidly and may become discoordinated," says Dr. Guitar.

By slowing down, you're modeling a way of speaking that your child is realistically able to achieve, adds Dr. Conture. "It also provides the child with sufficient time to smoothly and easily generate his own speech. Initially, in a conversation with your child, you may need to do this only for about five minutes. Then you can probably go back to a more typical speaking rate, provided you don't talk *too* rapidly."

Practice natural breathing. "A stutterer tries to superimpose speech over short, rapid, uneven breaths or speak while holding his breath," explains R. Gregory Nunn, Ph.D., a clinical psychologist and president of R.G. Nunn and Associates, a private clinic in San Diego. "We want him to get used to natural speech breathing."

Take a relaxed breath through the mouth, filling your lungs with a comfortable amount of air, and let it out slowly and easily, producing a deep, hollow sound. Practice this breathing pattern daily. Then try to maintain the deep breathing while you speak, letting the words come out easily as the smooth, even breath is being exhaled.

Take the pause that encourages. Don't be too hasty in responding to a child's comment or question, says Dr. Conture. "Pause for one or two seconds before you respond." This will underscore the calm, slow pace of conversation and make it easier for the stuttering child to keep up his end of the conversation.

Set aside a special time to chat. Life is busy for everyone these days, and parents can't always drop everything and engage in slow, measured conversation. "But it helps if a child knows that he has a certain time each day when the parent is going to listen to him. Even if you can set aside only five or ten minutes, that can compensate for the fact that life is too busy and rushed," says Dr. Guitar.

Let the child talk about his feelings. When you set aside some time to be with your child, let the child direct the conversation, says Dr. Guitar. Children who are going through a tough period of disfluency may have a lot of feelings and thoughts that have gone unexpressed, he notes. These quiet times with you, when the child is in charge, may give him the sense of security he needs to express himself. "It can really be magical if you create an environment where the child feels free to talk about feelings and where all feelings are considered okay and normal."

Use the salt shaker trick. A child who stutters may get shut out of fast-paced dinner conversations. One way to make things easier is to give dinner-table talk a special structure, says Dr. Guitar. "One family used a salt shaker that was passed around the table. If you had the salt shaker, it was your turn to talk and no one could interrupt you. This kind of structure is good for the stutterer because he doesn't feel he always has to struggle to get a word in."

Avoid "simultalk." "Try not to talk over the end of your child's utterance," says Dr. Conture. Though you sometimes may be tempted to finish your child's long, labored sentences, complete his thoughts or interrupt him in a rush to get the conversation moving, let him finish. Otherwise you could possibly make his stuttering worse.

Don't be so picky. Kids who stutter need to know that they don't have to be perfect, that they can make mistakes and still be okay. Many of these children worry more about how they talk than what they say.

"They worry about being perfect in talking, rather than just talking," says Dr. Conture. "Parents can help though, by not being so picky about everything—the child's room, his fingernails, his homework, his chores. Give the kid some slack," says

Dr. Conture, "so he can learn he can screw up and make mistakes and the world doesn't end."

Let speaking skills come naturally. Parents who are constantly correcting speech mistakes or stressing verbal skills can worsen their child's stuttering problems. "Take away any pressures," says Dr. Guitar. "Kids will develop language and speech skills on their own just by hearing conversation. They don't need to grow up in households where there's a lot of time spent learning vocabulary and the names of all the dinosaurs."

Make the teacher your ally. It's important that your child's teacher understand how to handle speech problems. "Giving oral reports, volunteering answers in class and reading aloud are all difficult things for the stuttering child. Don't ask the teacher to excuse your child from these activities," says Dr. Guitar, "but open up communication so the child feels comfortable talking to the teacher about it. Kids who stutter will have good days and bad days. Your child may want to strike a deal with the teacher that he's only called on when his hand is up, so his good days can be taken advantage of and his bad days forgiven."

TEETHING

When your baby begins to chew on everything in sight and starts drooling like Niagara Falls, it's a good guess the difficult teething months have officially begun.

Teeth begin to push through the gums when your baby is about six months old. This process can make the gums red and sensitive, and some babies will be fussy and irritable with every tooth that erupts. (Other babies, however, sail through the process with scarcely a whimper.)

The process continues until all 20 teeth come through, at about age 2½. Here's how to help your child deal with the discomfort from those emerging teeth.

Rub the gums. Just rubbing your baby's gums with your finger may make her feel better. And if you rub gently with a small gauze pad, you'll not only help relieve teething pain, but also clean your baby's mouth and get her used to the sensation of having her teeth cleaned, says John Bogert, D.D.S., pediatric dentist and executive director of the American Academy of Pediatric Dentistry in Chicago.

Offer soothing comfort. Sometimes a little tender care can ease the discomfort of a teething baby, says James F. Steiner, D.D.S., professor of clinical pediatrics and associate director of the Division of Pediatric Dentistry at Children's Hospital Medical Center in Cincinnati. Cuddling your baby, rocking him or walking with him often can make him feel better.

Supply a washcloth to chomp on. Give your baby a clean, wet washcloth to chew on, suggests Linda Jonides, R.N., a certified pediatric nurse practitioner in Ann Arbor, Michigan. If you chill the cloth in the refrigerator beforehand, it provides even more relief, by cooling those tender gums.

Ice is nice. Wrap a piece of ice in a bit of cotton cloth, says William Kuttler, D.D.S., a dentist in Dubuque, Iowa. "Rubbing this gently on the gums helps to numb them, and the pressure seems to feel good, too," he says. Be sure that the ice itself doesn't touch the gum, however, and that you keep the wrapped ice moving rather than holding it in one place.

Supply a teething ring. Teething rings with liquid centers intended for freezing are great for gum relief, says Dr. Steiner. But instead of freezing the ring, chill it in the refrigerator. "A child who holds a frozen teething ring against his gums can actually get frostbitten gums," explains Dr. Steiner. "Refrigerating them gets the rings cool enough to comfort the baby's gums without the potential harm from direct ice."

Consider an OTC pain reliever. If your baby is in serious discomfort or having trouble sleeping because of pain, call your doctor and ask about giving an over-the-counter pain reliever. Acetaminophen can help a baby who seems to be very uncomfortable, says F. T. Fitzpatrick, M.D., a pediatrician in private practice in Doylestown, Pennsylvania. Be sure to get a pain reliever that's specifically for infants, and check with your doctor for the correct dosage.

Try a gum preparation. Products that numb the gums, such as Orajel or Anbesol Baby Teething Gel can help ease gum pain, says Dr. Kuttler. Just follow directions on the package for use.

Mop up the drool. Drooling goes with teething. And clothing that has become wet from drooling can cause a rash, particularly on the neck and upper chest, says Dr. Fitzpatrick. To prevent this, change your child's clothing often, or keep a soft cloth or bib around your baby's neck to soak up the drool.

Protect your baby's face. Your child may need a bit of extra protection to keep from getting a rash on her face. "If your baby is drooling a great deal, put a coating of petroleum jelly around her mouth and chin, avoiding the lips," says Jonides.

TEMPER TANTRUMS

I t may happen at any time from about 14 months on. Your sweet cuddly baby suddenly becomes a raging monster, throwing a temper tantrum that reminds you of demonic possession. So you may be surprised to learn that temper tantrums are perfectly normal in humans of *all* ages, according to William Sobesky, Ph.D., assistant clinical professor of psychiatry at the University of Colorado Health Sciences Center and research psychologist at Children's Hospital, both in Denver.

"Everybody has tantrums. We don't ever outgrow them completely. As adults, we just get more subtle about expressing our displeasure," says Dr. Sobesky. "Two-year-olds, on the other hand, are more direct and challenging. They just let it all hang out."

Your role as parent of a child in his "terrible twos" is to teach him to control his rages, to learn some of that subtlety and restraint at which adults are so practiced. While the wild-eyed flailing and screaming that characterizes toddler tantrums usually diminishes—with help—by age three, some children have a more difficult time than others handling their tempers, Dr. Sobesky says.

But here are some techniques that can help you prevent the terrible twos from stretching into the terrible twelves.

Recognize and avoid flash points. Kids are more likely to lash out if they're tired, hungry or feeling rushed. "If you can predict those times when there will be problems, often you can work around them," says Dr. Sobesky.

You may be able to eliminate the dreaded checkout-line tantrums, for example, by not shopping when your child is hungry. A child who throws a fit during the morning "rush hour" around the house—when parents are headed for work, and older siblings for school—may need to get up a half hour earlier. "Know your child's bad times so you can prevent tantrums," says Dr. Sobesky.

Intervene early. It's a lot easier to stop a tantrum that's just starting than one in full bloom, says Dr. Sobesky. With young children, distraction often works. "Get them interested in something else, such as a toy or a game," he says. "Even getting silly or tickling them sometimes works."

Switch from "stop" to "go." Young children are more likely to respond to parental requests to do something—so-called go instructions—than to heed stop requests, says Mark Roberts, Ph.D., professor of psychology at Idaho State University in Pocatello. "So if your child is yelling and screaming, ask him to come to you instead of asking him to stop screaming. He's more likely to obey," says Dr. Roberts.

Name that emotion. A two-year-old may not be able to express in words—or even understand—his feelings of rage. To give him some control over his emotions, you have to give them a name, says Lewis P. Lipsitt, Ph.D., professor of psychology and medical science and founding director of the Child Study Center at Brown University in Providence, Rhode Island.

"Without making a judgment about his emotions, try reflecting back to the child what he is feeling, such as 'Maybe you're angry because you can't have a cookie,'" says Dr. Lipsitt. "Then make it clear that despite his feelings, there are boundaries to his behavior. Tell him, 'Even though you are angry, you must not yell and scream in the store.'" This helps to teach the child that there are certain situations where such behavior is not permitted.

Tell the truth about consequences. "With younger children, it's often helpful to explain the consequences of their bad behavior," says Dr. Lipsitt. "Explain things very simply: 'You are acting out of control and we don't allow that here. If you continue, you will have to go to your room.'"

Call time-out. "Chair time-outs are the discipline of choice for preschool children," says Dr. Roberts. He explains that a child who is having a tantrum should be required to sit on a chair that's next to a wall (away from all entertaining or dangerous objects) for a certain minimum period of time.

"From our research we know that less than one minute is not effective," says Dr. Roberts. Usually it takes between two and five minutes for the child to calm down, he says. You should not speak to the child during that time.

When the time is up and the child is calm, explain that his tantrums will not be tolerated. Then give a few suggestions for alternative behavior and allow things to return to normal, says Dr. Roberts.

Send the child to a time-out room. As many parents discover, an out-of-control toddler may not stay in a time-out chair. "In these situations, a brief, solitary time-out in a separate room can be helpful," says Dr. Roberts.

"If the child refuses to stay on the time-out chair, take the child by the arm and put him in his room," he suggests. "Close the door, hold it shut and wait for 60 seconds, listening carefully for 'dangerous' sounds—such as bouncing on the bed—that would require intervention. What usually happens is the child continues his tantrum at the door. After 60 seconds, carefully open the door, march the child back to the time-out chair and tell him to stay there and be quiet." You may have to do this three times or more before the child stays on the time-out chair, Dr. Roberts says. If a child aggressively and repeatedly refuses to stay on the chair during time-out, it's time to seek professional counsel, he adds.

Follow through on your warning. Once you tell a child that he'll have to take time-out in his room or in a chair, you must follow through consistently, adds Dr. Roberts. "Otherwise, it's like the story of the boy who cried wolf. Empty warnings don't accomplish anything. Children tune them out like background music."

Count to ten (or higher). It's not just the child who needs a time-out. You may need a break, too, especially if you are on the verge of losing control yourself after your child's temper outburst. "Just tell the child, 'I'm too upset with you right now. I need to settle down before we talk,'" suggests Dr. Sobesky.

"It's okay to be angry, but not okay to lose your temper," he says. "When parents yell and scream, they're not being good role models for their kids. If you do lose your temper, apologize, say, 'I'm sorry. That was my anger talking, not me.' Kids are very forgiving."

Counter fear with love. A child who is having a temper outburst is likely to be frightened by the intensity of his own out-of-control emotions. "Rage reactions scare the person who is angry," says Dr. Lipsitt. "In the midst of anger, children often feel like hitting—which is a particularly upsetting feeling for an older child."

The best way to bring these feelings under control is to express your love and concern. "Tell the child that everything is going to be all right soon," says Dr. Lipsitt, "and that his feelings are natural although not to be desired."

Conjure up a calm image. A useful tip to try with your child to keep his temper under control is to ask him to imagine something calming or actually, physically cool, says Thomas Olkowski, Ph.D., a clinical psychologist in private practice in Denver, Colorado.

"When the parents of one child I worked with tried this approach, the boy came up with a number of images to help him remember to 'keep cool.' Initially, he pictured himself sitting on a block of ice or going outside in a snowstorm. But he finally settled on a stuffed penguin as his imaginary reminder, because penguins always keep their cool."

If they can't cut it out, help them cut it back. A child who is temperamentally a hothead isn't going to change overnight, but she can make small changes daily, says Dr. Olkowski. "Let's say your child blows her stack three times a day. Pick a day and work with her to cut those outbursts down from three to two, just to give her a feeling of control. At that point she may think, 'Hey, I've done it at least once. Maybe I can do it again.' That gives her a sense of accomplishment."

THUMB-SUCKING

At 11, Brian was still sucking his thumb. Not all the time, and never at school or at friends' houses. But whenever he was lost in thought at home—whether studying the contents of the refrigerator or watching TV—his thumb would rise toward his mouth. And at night he'd fall asleep with that comforting thumb wedged firmly in place.

"I had visions of him going off to college sucking his thumb," says his mother. But as it turned out, he stopped even before junior high. Brian made the decision himself—and he succeeded with help from his parents.

Experts agree that sometimes thumb-sucking isn't a problem at all. "It's not a sign of insecurity—it's simply a habit," says Susan Heitler, Ph.D., a clinical psychologist in Denver. "It's a coping skill, much like pacing or cigarette smoking is to an adult," says Dr. Heitler. "If a child is agitated, it calms him down; if he's bored, it stimulates him."

If the child is under five, the best policy might be to ignore it. "If the child thumb-sucks only occasionally and it doesn't appear to be harming teeth or fingers, there's no need to do anything," says Stephen Goepferd, D.D.S., professor of pediatric dentistry and director of dentistry in the Division of Developmental Disabilities at the University Hospital School at the University of Iowa in Iowa City.

Problems can occur, however, if a child is vigorously thumb-sucking after age five, says Patrick Friman, Ph.D., associate professor of psychology at Creighton University Medical School in Omaha and the director of clinical research at Father Flanagan's Boys' Town, in Boys' Town, Nebraska. "The child may be at risk for buck teeth, malformation of the sucked fingers or thumbs and fungal infections under the nails," he says. And frequent thumb-sucking can take a social toll once a child starts school or preschool.

So if your youngster still has a thing for his thumb as school age approaches, you might want to take some positive action. Here are some steps that can help.

Can the nagging. No matter what your child's age, don't scold him about the habit. "If you've been nagging your child about his thumb-sucking, now is the time to call it quits," says Dr. Friman. Don't mention thumb-sucking unless the child brings it up. Particularly don't pull your child's thumb out of his mouth, he says. Sometimes just making a nonissue of thumb-sucking can help to cut back on it. If not, at least you've stopped making your child miserable about the habit.

Tune into your child's signals. If you want to gently steer your child away from thumb-sucking, take note of what's going on whenever your child's thumb goes in her mouth, says Dr. Heitler. "If your child automatically sucks her thumb when she's tired, hungry or bored, help her verbalize those feelings and look for other solutions," she suggests. "For instance, you can say to her, 'You must be feeling bored,' and then get her interested in a book or toy to take the place of her thumb."

Abandon cuddly props. Sometimes thumb-sucking and hugging a blanket or teddy bear are habits that are linked together, and your child automatically does one while doing the other. "Dragging around a blanket or teddy bear may trigger unnecessary daytime sucking," points out Dr. Heitler. If you make a rule that the blanket or teddy must stay in the child's bedroom, you'll likely cut down on thumb-sucking *outside* the bedroom.

Consider your timing. If you believe it's time for your child to actively try to break the thumb-sucking habit, pick a time when life is relatively calm, advises Dr. Goepferd. You probably won't get anywhere if there's been a death in the family or a serious illness, or if a divorce is in progress, he notes.

Give a reason to quit. If you want your child to quit because you think other children will make fun of him when he starts kindergarten, explain this. "It's easy for a child to see that he probably doesn't want to be sucking his thumb in front of all those other kids at school," says Dr. Heitler.

You can also explain that the pressure from the thumb could harm his teeth—and it helps if your pediatrician or dentist also mentions this. "It may take a heart-to-heart talk to convince your child that ending the habit is important," says Dr. Heitler.

Team up to stop the habit. Once your child is interested in quitting, discuss possible solutions together, says Dr. Friman. "That way, it's not something the parent is doing to the child, but rather something that the child is doing for himself." Parents can help with reminders, he says, but the child feels more in charge this way.

Pick a milestone for stopping. "It's often a good idea to tie the time for your child to stop sucking his thumb to a milestone or special event in her life, such as starting kindergarten, by New Year's or before summer vacation begins," says Dr. Heitler.

Once you've chosen the "stop" date, sit down with your child and design a colorful chart where you can record the hours or days he goes without sucking his thumb, suggests Dr. Heitler. This gives your child a sense of control, she says, and lets him see the progress he has made.

Reward success. "Build into your charting system little treats or rewards—something for your child to work toward in her endeavor to quit the habit," says William Kuttler, D.D.S., a dentist in Dubuque, Iowa, who has been treating children for more than 20 years. "It's very motivating."

He suggests giving a child a star for each day she gets through without sucking her thumb. You and the child can determine ahead of time how many stars she needs to collect before she earns a particular treat, such as a new toy.

Develop a warning system. "The hardest part of quitting is for the child to realize that his thumb is in his mouth, since it goes in by automatic pilot," says Dr. Heitler. You need a way to warn your child that the thumb is moving toward his mouth. Discuss it with your child, and pick something that will remind him what he's doing. A small adhesive bandage around the thumb may do the trick.

"If the plain bandage isn't enough, try putting a bit of vinegar on it," suggests Stuart Fountain, D.D.S., a dentist in Greensboro, North Carolina, and associate professor of endodontics at the University of North Carolina's Chapel Hill School of Dentistry. "The taste of the vinegar will remind your child that he's trying to quit."

Put a sock on it. If your child sucks her thumb when she's sleeping, even a bandage on the thumb may not stop it from going in the mouth. Instead, your child may want to put some gloves or socks over her hands while she sleeps, suggests Dr. Heitler.

Try thumb-painting. For the child who is trying to quit with little success, try Stopzit or a similar over-the-counter product, suggests Dr. Friman. These pharmacy products are safe for children, but contain bad-tasting ingredients that jolt the child's taste buds.

But be sure your child doesn't think of this as a punishment, warns Dr. Friman. "You can say to your child, 'Here's some medicine that can really help you when you forget and put your thumb in your mouth,'" he suggests. "The child gets the message that his parents aren't *making* him quit, they're *helping* him quit."

Offer an encouraging word. "Don't underestimate how difficult breaking this habit is for your child," says Dr. Heitler. "Thumb-sucking is a very rewarding habit, and doing without it creates a feeling of loss or emptiness. Much like what an adult feels when he gives up smoking." So be patient with your child, and offer frequent encouragement.

And even if your child quits, it will be easy for him to relapse during the first few weeks, points out Dr. Heitler. "Your child will have to work extra hard to guard against slipping back. It usually takes at least 30 days for the sucking impulse to subside."

TOILET TRAINING PROBLEMS

Though successful toilet training is often regarded as a milestone in a child's life, experts say parents spend far too much time worrying about it. And that can cause unnecessary problems.

Most kids are toilet trained by the time they're three, but it's not unusual—or abnormal—for a child of three and a half or four to still be untrained, notes George Sterne, M.D., clinical professor of pediatrics at Tulane University Medical School and a pediatrician in New Orleans. Boys seem to train later than girls, he adds.

If there's one word you should keep in mind about toilet training, say the experts, it's *relax*. "Toileting isn't something you can force," says Jeffrey Fogel, M.D., a pediatrician in Fort Washington, Pennsylvania, and staff physician at Chestnut Hill Hospital in Philadelphia.

But experts also say you can make toilet training easier for both you and your child if you follow these suggestions.

Buy a potty chair. "A potty chair can serve the same way as those little plastic lawn mowers parents buy for their kids. It's something that helps junior act like Daddy," says Thomas Bartholomew, M.D., pediatric urologist and assistant professor of surgery and urology at the University of Texas Health Science Center at San Antonio.

"Put the child's name on the chair and have him sit on it during a favorite activity—when he's hearing a story or watching a video, for example," adds Barton D. Schmitt, M.D., professor of pediatrics at The University of Colorado School of Medicine, director of consultative services at the Ambulatory Care Center at Children's Hospital of Denver and author of *Your Child's Health*. "You really ought to have the chair in place and the child enjoying it *before* you bring up the idea that this is also the place where he should go."

Step up to a potty seat. If your child is willing, you might start him on a potty seat that goes on top of the regular toilet seat, suggests Lottie Mendelson, R.N., a pediatric nurse practitioner in Portland, Oregon, and coauthor of *The Complete Book of Parenting*, with her husband, Robert. "Provide the child with a stool to help him get on and off," she suggests.

Or maybe he's ready for the big time. "Children who are strong enough can learn to go directly on the toilet by sitting backward—facing the water tank—to steady themselves," says Mendelson. Most kids want to try out the adult seat as soon as they're able, she points out.

Be a role model. Tell your child what you want him to do, but better yet, show him, suggests Dr. Bartholomew. For obvious reasons, it's best if the same-sex parent performs this particular duty. "It's like anything else—kids like to imitate their parents," says Dr. Bartholomew. "When they see you use the bathroom, they're going to want to use the bathroom."

Skip the transition. Though it may be tempting to use the diaperlike transition pants, Dr. Fogel doesn't advise it. "That sends a mixed message to kids," he says. "We're saying to them: 'You don't like those big bulky diapers? Fine, here's something that's thin, it's light, it looks just like underwear but you can pee and poop in it.' That takes away the big incentive of graduating from a diaper into the big-boy or big-girl pants." If protecting clothing and furniture is a high priority, and your child stays dry 95 percent of the time, you can buy training pants that are simply underwear with a padded crotch. They don't eliminate leaking, but they do reduce it, says Dr. Fogel.

Make a fuss over success. "Provide extra attention or play a special game if your child has a successful elimination in the toilet," says Cathleen Piazza, Ph.D., assistant professor of psychiatry at Johns Hopkins University School of Medicine and chief psychologist of the neurobehavioral unit at the Kennedy Krieger Institute in Baltimore. She suggests that you give your child a particular toy, stickers or a favorite food item as a toilet training reward.

Find out what motivates your child. "You can give children reasons to use the potty, but they have to be reasons that matter to them," says Dr. Fogel. He suggests that you listen to your child's cues. "For example, if your kid sees the big-boy underwear in the store and says, 'Oh, look at that, the Ninja Turtles,' you can say, 'Well, when you're fully dry during the day you can have them, too.' That way, the motivation is coming from him," says Dr. Fogel.

Don't let the bathroom become a battleground. Don't ever fight with your child about using the toilet. "Fighting is counterproductive," says Dr. Fogel. Instead, think of toileting as a skill that will come naturally, given some time and patience. "It's like any other developmental milestone," notes Dr. Fogel. "A child has to want to do it and be able to do it. Just as you can't force a child to walk, to crawl or to roll over, you can't make him use the toilet."

Parents who try to force the issue risk getting locked into a "battle of the bowels" that could, if unresolved, require the help of a professional therapist, says Dr. Sterne.

If he starts withholding, back off. It's a clear sign that a child is not ready to use the toilet if he begins to withhold stools, says Dr. Sterne.

"If that happens, back off," he says. "Say, 'You don't want to use the potty? Okay. If you want to wear your diaper, wear your diaper. I can see you're uncomfortable about letting go.'"

Withholding can also occur because of fear. "Some children are afraid of falling into the toilet," says Dr. Sterne. "Others may get scared if you flush the toilet while they're still sitting on it. You may need to give your child more time to get used to the whole idea."

TOOTH CARE

A clean report—"No cavities!"—is quite possible these days, according to Luke Matranga, D.D.S., president of the Academy of General Dentistry and chairman of the Department of Comprehensive Dental Care at Creighton University Dental School in Omaha.

Of course, nothing can substitute for good dental care, and most dentists recommend visits every six months after the age of two. But along with the dentist's attention, excellent at-home habits can go a long way toward preventing cavities. Here's how.

Skip baby's bedtime bottle. Lull your baby to sleep with a lullaby—or a bottle filled with clear water—instead of a bottle with milk or juice, says Dr. Matranga. When your baby falls asleep with milk or juice in his mouth, the sugars in those beverages can decay teeth when they combine with plaque, a "film" on the teeth that encourages bacterial growth. In fact, most cases of extensive infant tooth decay are known as "baby bottle syndrome," he says.

Clean your baby's gums. Good dental habits start early—even before teeth come in. "You should get your child used to mouth care by wiping her gums with a moist, soft cloth right after she eats," says William Kuttler, D.D.S., a dentist in Dubuque, Iowa, who has been treating children for more than 20 years.

Direct the brushing. Start brushing teeth as soon as they appear, using a round-tipped, soft-bristle baby's toothbrush *without* toothpaste, says Jed Best, D.D.S., a pediatric dentist and assistant clinical professor of pediatric dentistry at Columbia University School of Dentistry in New York City. Continue to assist your child with brushing as long as he needs it, Dr. Best advises.

"A good rule of thumb is that if your child is dexterous enough to tie his own shoes, he can probably brush his own teeth," says Dr. Best. "Until then, you can let your child do the best he can, then go over any spots he's missed."

Let your child choose the toothbrush. When your child is old enough to do the brushing, she's more likely to enjoy it if she has a toothbrush she likes—one festooned with cartoon characters, for example. "As long as the toothbrush is appropriate for a child—with a small head and soft, round-tipped, nylon bristles—your child can select it on her own," says Dr. Matranga.

Find fluoridated toothpaste. After your child has six or seven teeth, it's time for her to start using toothpaste. "Choose one that is fluoridated, but not tartar-control," advises Cynthia Fong, a registered dental hygienist and assistant clinical professor in the Department of General and Hospital Dentistry at the University of Medicine and Dentistry of New Jersey/New Jersey Dental School in Newark. Some tartar-control products can be abrasive, she explains, and tartar buildup isn't a common problem in children. Also, make sure your child knows which tube of toothpaste is exclusively hers.

Brush twice a day. Many people—children and adults alike—do only a perfunctory job of brushing. It takes time to remove plaque and debris from teeth, and once a day isn't enough. "Your child should brush his teeth for two to three minutes at least twice a day," says Dr. Best. One brushing should be just before bed, so food particles or plaque don't remain on your child's teeth overnight.

Introduce flossing early. As soon as your toddler has two back teeth that touch, it's time to start daily flossing. But you'll be in charge of this task for quite a while—likely until your child is seven or eight, says Dr. Best. "This takes even more manual dexterity than brushing," he explains.

Sit to floss. The easiest way to floss your child's teeth is to sit behind her while she's standing or kneeling, with her head in your lap. "Now she's in a position similar to that in a dentist's chair," says Fong. This will let you reach your child's teeth more easily and see what you're doing.

Try a mechanical toothbrush or an irrigator. The buzz of a special mechanical appliance can make daily tooth care more appealing to some children—and can cut the time required as well. "Electric or battery-operated toothbrushes do an excellent job of cleaning the teeth, in about half the time of a manual brushing," says Dr. Matranga. Oral irrigators that shoot a stream of water onto the teeth help get food particles out from between teeth. But parents shouldn't assume that oral irrigation is a substitute for brushing and flossing, he says.

Set a good example. If your child sees you brushing and flossing your teeth and choosing snacks that are healthy for your teeth, it's more likely that she will do the same. "Good tooth care is a learned behavior," says Dr. Kuttler. "If parents put a high value on their own dental health, their children are much more likely to want to do the same."

Grasp at straws. If your child drinks soda or juice, she can minimize the potential tooth damage by drinking from a straw. The straw directs the beverage past the teeth, so they aren't "bathed" in sugars. "A straw limits the time the drink is in contact with the teeth," says Dr. Kuttler, "so less damage is done."

Rinse with water. After your child has had a snack or a meal, have him swish plain water in his mouth. "This removes some of the loose food particles and sugar," says Fong. Brushing is better, notes Fong, but when a toothbrush isn't available, swishing is better than nothing.

TV ADDICTION

Six-year-old Alex's family was planning an extra-special cross-country trip in a camper. When Alex found out there would be no television for the entire three weeks, he couldn't believe it. "But what will I *do*?" he squawked.

Whenever ten-year-old Tracy enters her room, she turns on her TV set. It's as automatic as flipping on the light switch. Whether she is doing homework, playing with friends or talking on the phone, her TV is always on.

Both Alex and Tracy are TV addicts. In some ways, they are as dependent on the flickering screen images as many grown-ups are on cigarettes or alcohol. And the consequences can be serious.

As many studies have shown, children who watch a lot of television are fatter and less fit and have higher cholesterol levels than kids who watch less. Some experts think excessive tube-watching may even foster a more accepting attitude toward violence and promote aggressive behavior.

If you're concerned that your child is watching too much television, here are some tips for cutting back.

Log in those viewing hours. "Keep a record of how much television your child actually watches," suggests Nicholas A. Roes, president of the Education Guild and author of *Helping Children Watch TV*. You may be quite surprised at how many hours per week are spent that way. Once you know the extent of the problem, you'll be in a better position to institute needed changes, says Roes.

Short-circuit the electronic babysitter. "Don't get in the habit of using television as a babysitter, no matter how busy you are," says Marie Winn, author of *Unplugging the Plug-In Drug*. Instead, come up with some *active* pastimes your child can pursue when you're not available to supervise.

You might provide a wide variety of drawing materials, for instance, or purchase some simple musical instruments for your child to play with on his own. If you read to your child—and do a lot of reading yourself—you'll encourage your child to be entertained by books as well as television.

Map out a week's worth of watching. "Go through the channel listings with your child each weekend and select programs for the coming week that you would feel comfortable having her watch," says Carole Lieberman, M.D., a Beverly Hills psychiatrist, media consultant and assistant clinical professor of psychiatry at the University of California, Los Angeles. "Choose programs that are educational and nonviolent, that espouse the kinds of values you want your child to have."

If the show is part of a series, she suggests you watch at least one episode with your child to make sure it's really suitable. *Important:* As soon as the chosen program is over, and before your child can get hooked on the one that happens to follow, turn the set off, Dr. Lieberman says.

Take a day off. "Designate a single day every week as No-TV Day," suggests Winn. "Some families do this on Saturday or Sunday as part of their Sabbath observance." Explain that everyone—Mom and Dad included—will just have to find more creative ways to fill their free time on that day.

Make time for homework. Try the "no TV on school nights" rule, which is the easiest one to enforce, according to Winn. Discuss the rule first in a family meeting, so your child knows why you feel it's so important.

"Children won't necessarily watch TV all weekend to make up for what they've missed on week nights," says Winn. In fact, because they haven't fallen into the viewing habit during the week, they'll be more likely to look to other leisure activities once Saturday rolls around.

Try a TV Turn-Off Week. Occasionally, you can present your children with the challenge of keeping the set turned off for a whole week, suggests Winn, who has organized TV Turn-offs around the country. "That's when you'll see how dependent your family is on television." The insight may be sobering, but it could help you to set limits in the future, she points out.

Expect withdrawal symptoms: Your kids may beg to watch "just one" favorite show. But hold firm.

"Just be sure you present it as a scientific experiment or an adventure—absolutely not as a punishment," says Winn. "As additional motivation, think up a reward for the end of the week. You might decide to take a special family trip or purchase a new game or other play equipment."

Don't let TV intrude on sleep time. Set a regular bedtime for your child that doesn't change from night to night depending on when certain television programs end, advises Bobbi Vogel, Ph.D., a family counselor in Woodland Hills, California, and director of the Adolescent Outpatient Program at Tarzana Treatment Center in Tarzana. And don't put a TV set in your child's bedroom, unless you want to completely lose control of how and when she uses it.

Switch off background temptation. Discourage your child from leaving the television on as background noise, advises Dr. Vogel. "It's too visually stimulating," she says. Before you know it, she could be watching instead of just listening. If she likes to hear something while she's drawing or doing other things, she can play a record or listen to the radio instead.

INDEX

Note: <u>Underscored</u> page references indicate boxed text.

A

A and D ointment, for diaper
rash, 44
Acetaminophen, as treatment for
chicken pox, 16, 18
croup, 32
ear infections, 45-46
fever, 58
growing pains, 62
measles, 73
mumps, 78
teething, 110-11
Addiction, TV, 126-28
Additives, food, attention
problems and, <u>6</u>
Aggressiveness, 1-4
Alarm clock, for bed-wetting, 12
Alarms, bed, for bed-wetting, 13
Alcohol rubdown, for fever, 59
Allergies, milk, ear infections
from, 47
Alpha-Keri body oil, for dry skin,
89
Amblyopia, 65-68
Anbesol Baby Teething Gel, for
teething pain, 111
Anger
aggressiveness and, 1
temper tantrums and, 115
Anorexia nervosa, 52
Antibiotic ointment, as treatment
for
chicken pox, 18-19
impetigo, 63
Antibiotics, oral, as treatment for
ear infections, 45
impetigo, 63
Antihistamines, as treatment for

chicken pox, 19
impetigo, 64
motion sickness, 77
nighttime coughing, 24
prickly heat, 90
Antinausea medications, for
motion sickness, 77
Anxiety. *See also* Fear(s)
school refusal and, 91-95
separation, 96-97
Appetite
eating problems and, 52
with fever, 60
Arguing, and sibling rivalry, 102-5
Aspirin, Reye's syndrome and, <u>18</u>,
58
Attention problems, 5-8
A-200, for head lice, 69
Aveeno Bath Treatment, as
treatment for
chicken pox, 17
prickly heat, 89

B

Baby bottle syndrome, 123
Baby wipes, diaper rash from, 43
Baker's P & S Liquid, for cradle
cap, 27
Baking soda, as treatment for
chicken pox, 17
prickly heat, 89
Balmex ointment, for diaper rash,
44
Bandage, for thumb-sucking, 119
Bathing, as treatment for
chicken pox, 17
diaper rash, 44
fever, 59

for nighttime coughing, 24-25
Cradle cap, 26-27
Crankiness, 28-29
Critical thinking skills,
     development of, 3
Crossed eyes, 67
Croup, 30-32
Crying, 33-37
     with colic, 20-22
     from separation anxiety, 96-97
     stridor with, 30

D

Dawdling, 38-41
     meaning of, 40
Dehydration, from fever, 74
Dessert, eating problems and, 51-52
Dextromethorphan, as treatment
     for
     measles cough, 74
     nighttime coughing, 24-25
Diaper rash, 42-44
     impetigo from, 64
Diapers
     cloth, 42
     disposable, 42, 44
     toilet training and, 121
Diarrhea, with fever, 59
Discipline
     for aggressiveness, 1-2
     for refusal to wear eye patch,
          67-68
     for sibling rivalry, 103
     for temper tantrums, 113-14
Dramamine, for motion sickness,
     77
Drooling, from teething, 110, 111
Drugs. *See specific drugs*
Dry skin, in newborns, 88-89

E

Ear drops, for ear infections, 46

Ear infections, 45-47
Eating. *See also* Bottlefeeding;
     Breastfeeding; Feeding
     colic and, 21-22
     problems with, 48-52
     with fever, 60
Electrolyte replacement fluid, as
     treatment for
     croup, 32
     diarrhea, 59
Epiglottitis, 31
Excitement, bed-wetting and, 11
Exercise(s)
     relaxation, for overcoming fears,
          55-56
     stream-interruption, for bladder
          control, 12-13
Expectorants, for bronchitis, 15
Eye contact
     for attention problems, 7
     with dawdlers, 41
Eye patching, for lazy eye, 65-68
Eye problems
     crossed eyes, 67
     lazy eye, 65-68
     with measles, 74

F

Fabric softeners, diapers and, 42
Fantasizing, aggressiveness and, 4
Fear(s), 53-56
     night terrors and nightmares,
          80-84
     of school, 91-95
     temper tantrums and, 115
Feeding. *See also* Bottlefeeding;
     Breastfeeding; Eating
     crying and, 35-36
     schedules 21-22
Fever. *See also* Temperature
     acetaminophen for, 16, 18, 32,
          58, 73